ENDORSEMENTS

"Beth Kennedy has written a beautiful, Spirit-breathed invitation into the heart of God. In *I Am God's Happy Place*, she gently reminds us that we are not only loved—we are delighted in. With heartfelt honesty and biblical insight, Beth leads us into a deeper awareness of the One who sees us, knows us, and desires to walk with us in every moment of our day.

"This book is filled with the fragrance of intimacy with Jesus. Through each chapter, Beth invites readers into a lifestyle of stillness and connection with God—not through striving, but by resting in His love. It's a healing message for a busy, distracted world: that we are God's happy place, not because of what we do, but because of who we are to Him.

"Whether you're just beginning to explore the voice of God or longing to deepen your walk with Him, this book will stir your heart, ignite your faith, and awaken you to the joy of living daily in the light of His love. I wholeheartedly recommend it."

Katherine Ruonala
Senior leader, Glory City Church, Brisbane
www.katherineruonala.com

"Beth is an outstanding writer, a good friend, and someone I respect deeply. This book is a masterpiece—beautifully written and overflowing with the revelation of God's profound love for you.

"Each of the twelve chapter titles drew me in, stirring a desire to read more and discover more. From the very first lines of the Introduction, I was captivated by Beth's message. Throughout the book, she weaves in remarkable "God Is Good Stories" that bring her words to life. Her opening story about Ethan moved me to tears as I felt the overwhelming presence of God's love.

"This book is filled with practical wisdom. Beth carries a breaker anointing—her words release life, hope, and encouragement with a seamless flow that draws you into deeper encounters with God's extraordinary love.

"I wholeheartedly recommend this book—not just for you, but for everyone you care about. It's a gift worth sharing. Blessings to be seen, known, and heard! Blessings to feel accepted and belong! Blessings to know—you are God's happy place!"

Joseph Peck, M.D.
Founder of Empower 2000 and The Time Doctor
www.empower2000.com

"Many talk about our identity in Christ, but what does that mean? Beth writes about how to walk with God and find your true identity as God's person, loved and cherished. She tells stories that reveal God's goodness and generous love. She shares her own experiences of walking with God. Some might find her very much 'out there!' Keep going, I say, because this book is one of those rare gems where someone who genuinely walks with God shares what it is like. Precious stuff."

Rev'd Philippa Lohmeyer-Collins
Associate minister, St Paul's Cathedral, Melbourne, Australia

"Beth Kennedy has crafted a book that breathes with the nearness of God. *I Am God's Happy Place* carries an anointing to disarm shame and awaken connection. With every chapter, Beth guides the reader into experiential awareness of God's intentional pursuit and unwavering delight. Her stories and biblical examples inspire and model a lifestyle of sensitivity to the Spirit in everyday moments. Beyond solid and engaging concepts, Beth paves a pathway for true communion.

"I know Beth as a true practitioner of presence, and her writing carries the resonance of someone who knows the Father's heartbeat. Expect to encounter God's affection in ways that surprise you and transform how you see yourself—and others."

Dan McCollam
Author, trainer, and co-founder of Prophetic Company,
Bethel School of the Prophets, the SQ Institute, and Finders

"Beth Kennedy invites us to lay down striving and step into something far better: awareness of the God who is already near. This book is soaked in presence. With gentle power, she reminds us that we are not called to be impressive, we are called to be present. Each chapter feels like an invitation to breathe, abide, and remember that we are, and always have been, God's happy place."

Ian Carroll
Founder, Sacred Space Coaching, author and itinerant

"In a culture that often celebrates performance over presence, it's easy to forget that God's delight in us isn't rooted in what we do, but in who we are to Him. *I Am God's Happy Place* is a beautiful and timely reminder that the Spirit of God has made His home within us—and He actually enjoys being there. Beth Kennedy weaves Scripture, personal story, and practical activation into a message that calls us back to the joy of simply being loved. This book doesn't just tell you who you are—it helps you feel it. It's an invitation to live from the inside out, fully embraced and fully known."

Bethany Hicks
Co-founder of Prophetic Company
Author of *Own Your Assignment*, *The God Connection*,
The Power in a Name, and *Seasons and Assignments*

"Beth is a friend, faithful church member, and a powerful prophet. She doesn't write from a theoretical posture, but from years of daily encounters which she so warmly weaves into each chapter. While you will be equipped to hear God's voice in the everyday ordinary, much more than that you will be transformed in how God thinks about you in the process. And how does one put a value on that? Dig in, take your time, and let God love you through these pages."

Fini de Gersigny
Senior pastor, Jubilee Church Sydney
www.jubilee.org.au

"It is a rare privilege to introduce a book that so tenderly and powerfully speaks to the deepest longings of the human heart. In a world that often feels fragmented and impersonal, Beth's book is a gentle, persistent reminder that we are not alone, that we are seen, known, and cherished by a loving God.

"From the very first lines, Beth invites us to embark on a journey—not just through her own stories, but into the greater story of God's relentless pursuit of relationship with each one of us. Her words echo a truth that resonates across every culture and generation: we were made to belong. This longing for acceptance and connection is not a flaw or a weakness, but a reflection of our original design, a sacred imprint of our Creator's heart.

"What makes this book so compelling is Beth's willingness to share her life with honesty and vulnerability. Through her "God Is Good Stories," she brings biblical truths to life, demonstrating that God's love is not a distant ideal but a living reality, experienced in the ordinary and extraordinary moments of our everyday lives. Her testimonies are more than anecdotes; they are invitations for us to look for God's goodness in our own stories.

"Beth's approach is refreshingly practical. She doesn't simply offer inspiration—she equips her readers with tools to hear God's voice, to pray with purpose, and to respond to His love in tangible ways. The reflection questions and action steps at the end of each chapter are not just exercises; they are opportunities for transformation, designed to help us move from head knowledge to heart experience.

"As you read, you will find yourself drawn into a conversation with God—a conversation marked by kindness, grace, and the gentle assurance that you are, indeed, His delight. Beth's hope, and mine, is that you will discover afresh how extravagantly you are loved, and that this revelation will become the foundation for every aspect of your life.

"So, I invite you to read with an open heart. Allow these pages to speak to your deepest needs and to awaken new hope within you. May you encounter the God who calls you His happy place, and may you find, in these words, the courage to step fully into the life and love He has prepared for you.

Gary Grant
Senior spiritual leader, Friends First Community, Melbourne

EXPERIENCING GOD'S
ACCEPTANCE, **ATTENTION**,
AND **DELIGHT** EVERY DAY

I am GOD'S HAPPY PLACE

☺

BETH KENNEDY

FOREWORD BY JAMES W. GOLL

Copyright © 2025 Beth Kennedy

ISBN: 978-0-6456265-2-0 (print)
ISBN: 978-0-6456265-3-7 (e-book)

No part of this book may be reproduced, stored in a retrieval system or transmitted in any form or by any means – electronic, mechanical, photocopy, recording or any other – except for brief quotations, without permission in writing from the author at www.verveministries.com.

Unless otherwise marked, Scripture quotations are from the Holy Bible, New International Version®, Copyright ©1973, 1978, 1984, 2011 by Biblica, Inc.® Used by permission. All rights reserved worldwide. Scripture quotations marked NKJV are from the New King James Version®. Copyright © 1982 by Thomas Nelson. Used by permission. All rights reserved. Scripture quotations marked TPT are from The Passion Translation®. Copyright © 2017, 2018, 2020 by Passion & Fire Ministries, Inc. Used by permission. All rights reserved. The PassionTranslation.com. Scripture quotations marked KJV are from the King James Version of the Bible, public domain. Scripture quotations marked ESV are from the Holy Bible, English Standard Version. ESV® Text Edition: 2016. Copyright © 2001 by Crossway Bibles, a publishing ministry of Good News Publishers. Scripture quotations marked NLT are from the Holy Bible, New Living Translation, copyright © 1996, 2004, 2015 by Tyndale House Foundation. Used by permission of Tyndale House Publishers, Inc., Carol Stream, Illinois 60188. All rights reserved.

Cover by Yvonne Parks at PearCreative.ca
Typesetting by Christy Distler at AvodahEditorialServices.com

CONTENTS

Foreword	13
Introduction	15
1. God Sees, Hears, and Knows	19
2. Feeling God's Attention	31
3. God Encounters Are an Invitation to More	43
4. The Command to Be Still	57
5. The No-Striving Zone	71
6. Abiding in My God Space	85
7. Present to God	105
8. Changed in His Presence, Chosen for His Purpose	123
9. Being the Fragrance of Christ	139
10. God Calls Me by Name	155
11. Lovers and Workers	169
12. God's Love Never Ends	183
Do You Know Jesus?	201
Notes	205
Acknowledgments	209
About the Author	211

To the Trinity—Father, Son, and Holy Spirit—whose love never ends.

And to those who have a hankering for more.

His goodness knows no limits, and His joy delights! Life with God is an adventure, not a job description. It's a pleasure to set out on the Way.

> *"I am looking for someone to share in an adventure that I am arranging."*
> *–Gandalf, in* The Hobbit *by J.R.R. Tolkien*

FOREWORD

Over the years, I've polled people on what they believe is the primary ministry of the Holy Spirit. I always get correct and common answers, such as distributing gifts, bringing conviction, speaking truth, bearing witness, and producing fruit.

Sometimes I continue to probe to see what else these wonderful believers might say. More answers come pouring out, including exposing deception, revealing the Father's heart, glorifying Jesus, magnifying the Word of God, guiding people, and other insightful replies.

All these answers are brilliant, but incomplete. Not one time have I ever heard the answer I was looking for. What do you say is the primary ministry of the Holy Spirit? John 16:13 (NASB) states, "But when He, the Spirit of truth, comes, He will guide you into all the truth; for He will not speak on His own, but *whatever He hears*, He will speak; and He will disclose to you what is to come" (emphasis added). Before He speaks, He listens.

One of the most overlooked ministries of the Holy Spirit is that of listening, as He listens before He speaks. It seems to me that we need to take some lessons from the nature and character of the Holy Spirit!

This may seem like a peculiar segue to a foreword for a wonderful, new friend's book with an intriguing subject entitled *I Am God's Happy Place*. This makes sense, as listening and speaking are fundamentally relational. Huh? You heard me correctly! This is not just a *ministry* of the Holy Spirit; it is about having an intimate *relationship* with the Holy Spirit.

James 1:19 (NLT) gives us some additional insight. "Understand this, my dear brothers and sisters: You must all be quick to listen, slow to speak." Good communication is grounded in good listening skills. Good relationships are based in a two-way interaction. We must learn to be present in the moment in order to hear a current word of the Holy Spirit. If not, we might be living out of yesterday's word instead receiving the revelatory diet that comes from resting in His presence.

Listening is not passivity; listening is an activity from an attentive spirit waiting for the relational initiative of a loving Creator. It is responsive. It is intuitive. It is knowing. It is wonderful! It is my happy place!

I am thrilled to see new voices, such as Beth Kennedy, that are arising in this hour of the global harvest. I am glad to see that they are not religious but relational. They encourage God encounters to emerge that are grounded in the rich soil of God's Word. I am so grateful to see another generation coming forth that knows the necessity of Psalm 46:10, "Be still, and know that I am God." Indeed, this is the imprint that I desire to release to others. This is a divine key of multiplication where the Spirit of wisdom and revelation comes to rest upon an individual for such a time as this.

This is when our desires align with His, and transformation begins. Oh, how majestic is the love of Christ. This is when He becomes my Happy Place as I am His. Amen and AMEN!

James W. Goll
God Encounters Ministries
GodEncounters.com

INTRODUCTION

We each have an innate desire to be seen, known, and heard. We all need acceptance and a place where we can belong. This sense of belonging affirms who we are and will even give us some understanding of why we exist. We can see this need manifest through the creation of clubs, societies, cliques, and even gangs. What many don't realize is that this need reflects our original design: we are created for a relationship with God and for relationship with others.

Simply put, we were created to belong to the family of God, and from this place of family, ideally, we experience loving acceptance where we can thrive. From the moment of deception in the garden of Eden until today, God has been calling each of us back to Himself, back into His family, through His Son, Jesus Christ.

To personalize it, I can say without pause that God has cast His eyes across the earth and looked upon *you*. Delight wells up from deep within His heart as He gazes upon *you*. Without reserve I know that God created you *from* His heart of love, *for* His heart of love, and His love for you will never end. You are His beloved, created with a purpose in mind, the fulfillment of which will bring you the greatest joy in life. And like any good father, He delights as He sees you step into all He's designed for you. To catch the smallest glimpse of His

INTRODUCTION

heart is to know no bounds to His love—*for you*. Without doubt, *you* are God's happy place!

ABOUT THIS BOOK

In each chapter of this book, I explore a single theme. Scattered throughout are some of my personal testimonies—or as I like to call them, *God Is Good Stories*. They demonstrate the truths revealed in each chapter and highlight that they are not mere concepts but scripturally based, lived truths with real-life application.

Of course, the importance of the *God Is Good Stories* should never be underestimated. In Revelation 12:11 we're told that we triumph over the enemy (the accuser) by the blood of the Lamb and *the power of our testimony*, and that we do not love our lives "so much as to shrink from death." Our own stories with God—our testimonies—carry great power to transform those with whom we share them. As you read the stories contained in this book, allow the Holy Spirit to speak to you. And if they challenge you in any way, ask God why.

I hope you'll recognize yourself in these stories and start to see how profoundly God loves both you and those around you as you go about your day. God is no respecter of persons (Acts 10:34), so as you read, ask Him for anything you would like to experience in your own life.

Within these chapters are also keys to how you can hear from God for yourself and for others. Please read with ears to hear, eyes to see, and a heart to know. If you do, I promise you will be inspired and supernaturally empowered and equipped. You will glean ways of wisdom on how to engage with the Lord and engage with others throughout your day. You'll see hints for how to pray for others, and you'll learn what the Holy Spirit's nudges might feel like and how you can respond to them.

At the end of each chapter are questions for you to consider and suggested action steps to take. You will grow as you engage in the process, but please never feel pressure to perform. These questions are meant to help you contemplate and recognize for yourself mindsets and

INTRODUCTION

beliefs that might be limiting your understanding of God's goodness in your life. We can all afford to be more extravagant in our view of how much He adores us without ever risking over-exaggeration. As you contemplate God's loving-kindness, He will encounter you, and with every encounter you will discover more about Him and yourself. Never forget that you are His masterpiece, "created in Christ Jesus to do good works, which God prepared in advance for us to do" (Ephesians 2:10).

Following the questions is the invitation to respond to the revelation with an action step. Every revelation demands a response from us, for how can we not respond to a love so pure, enduring, and powerful. Just as a child who smiles through a crowd demands a smile in return, so, too, does the lover of your soul demand a response. Love will always compel us further and deeper into Love's embrace. As you take these action steps, you will catch and secure insight into *your* world.

Then at the close of each chapter are suggested prayers. I invite you to pray with me, understanding that your agreement and action will cause activation and acceleration in your life.

I hope that by its conclusion this book will have thoroughly convinced you of God's endless love for you and those around you. With this foundation, when the rains come and the winds blow, you will stand firm in the knowledge that God is good and that you are forevermore His happy, happy place!

1

GOD SEES, HEARS, AND KNOWS

*She gave this name to the Lord who spoke to her:
"You are the God who sees me."*
Genesis 16:13

IN THE EARLY days of learning how to hear God's voice, I'd already started praying for people as I felt led. At the time of the story I'm about to tell, I was hungry to grow. So whenever and wherever I could, I asked God to highlight who He wanted me to write a word for as I went about my day. With two small children, that usually meant someone in my neighborhood.

One day I was at the local hair salon when God instantly highlighted one of the hairdressers, a young man I'll call Ethan. I could sense Ethan's desire to be accepted. With accentuated speech, behavior, makeup, clothes, and jewelry—on his fingers, through his ears, and in his nose—he jingle-jangled and caught the salon lights as he wildly gestured and talked. While I could feel his desperate need for love, it was Ethan's striving attitude that spoke the loudest to me. Everything about him was saying *Accept me as I am!* I leaned in and asked God if this was the issue I was to address. God's reply was spontaneous and firm: *That is none of your business. I will show you what I want you to say to him.*

Adequately rebuked, I turned to God's heart for this young man. He showed me an internal vision—a moving picture in my mind's imagination. I saw Ethan dancing and singing on rooftops with an open umbrella. Arms raised, face in a smile, he was spinning and leaping building to building, brimming with joy. The vision reminded me of the "Step in Time" dance scene in the film *Mary Poppins*. I still see it as I write now, and at its recollection, I always smile. I could sense the Father's sheer delight: *That's My boy. Can you see him? I adore him. Look at him go. Look at him go. Isn't he amazing? Isn't he gorgeous?*

I wrote as led, and then I nervously approached Ethan and said, "I'm a Christian, and I'm learning how to hear from God for others. He highlighted you, and I've written out something from Him, for you. Could I share it with you, please?"

His response was immediate. "Absolutely!"

I pulled out my paper and carefully described the internal picture I'd seen. Then I told him, "God sees you joyfully dance on those rooftops and thoroughly delights in you. He gets you, and He adores who you are. He wants you to be thoroughly you. The Father loves you, and He wants you to know you're wonderful."

I can't recall it all, but I shared so much more, glancing up as I read and seeing Ethan gently crying.

"Oh, I love this," he said when I was finished. "I thought God didn't even like me, let alone love me. In fact, I thought He hated me. I thought I wasn't acceptable to Him. This is so good. Can I keep that, please?"

I gave him the paper and asked if I could pray the blessing in. He immediately agreed, and as we stood there in the salon, I prayed the Father's heart for him. Then after the prayer, we both wiped tears from our eyes. Ethan looked at the paper again, then carefully folded it as he walked away to the back room of the salon. Now feeling awkward, I sat down. I'd been nervous, and it would take some time for me to settle.

Only later did I learn the full effect of this word, but I soon knew its immediate impact—and in hindsight it's rather amusing. As I was getting my hair cut, Ethan remained in the back room. But one by one, several other hairdressers went back there, too, and then reemerged and stared at me. Apparently I'd caused quite the spectacle.

I watched all this take place in the mirrors around me and felt conspicuous. But what mattered was that Ethan had encountered the God who sees, and he was letting others know. The creator of the universe had seen him at his workplace and made it abundantly clear that He saw, knew, and loved him. In an instant, Ethan felt valued by a God he didn't yet know but who undeniably knew and loved him. As this realization penetrated his heart, he was telling others about the God who saw him, about the God who cared.

I'll share what happened next later in this chapter, but for now, let's turn to Genesis 15 and 16, where God encounters a young servant girl named Hagar who realizes that God is in fact the God who truly sees.

AMID THE MESS A PROMISE CONCEIVED

At seventy-five years of age, Abram (not yet called Abraham) receives a promise from God. He's told that despite his advanced age, he will father a generational legacy. God takes him outside and says, "Look up at the sky and count the stars—if indeed you can count them. . . . So shall your offspring be" (Genesis 15:5).

The promise takes time to eventuate, and so by the time Abram is eighty-six, there's great tension between the promise revealed and the promise yet to be fulfilled. In her own wisdom, Abram's wife, Sarai (not yet called Sarah) takes matters into her own hands. No child has been forthcoming, and time is ticking along! The promises of God seem to tarry, and so Sarai determines to help God with His plan. She speaks to her husband about their servant girl, Hagar, and suggests he sleep with her so they might have an heir.

Now, in our modern Judeo/Christian mindset, this sounds like a dreadful plan. But not so much for them. In their culture, it was common practice for a female servant to become a secondary wife, and any child born from this union was seen as the first wife's child.

Therefore, a child born to Abram and Hagar became a child born to Abram and Sarai. Any such child was a rightful heir, supplanted only by a child born from the first wife.

Sarai may have felt this plan solved her perceived barrenness, but it sadly missed the point. She simply needed to wait for God's promise to be fulfilled. The biggest issue was that her plan worked brilliantly.

Hagar conceives quickly, and as her belly grows, so, too, does her disrespect for Sarai. It would be fair to suppose Sarai becomes jealous of Hagar, and I have no doubt that her feelings are exacerbated by her slave's outright disrespect (16:4). She complains about Hagar to Abram, who simply washes his hands of the mess by telling Sarai to do with Hagar however she pleases (16:6).

Now, remember, as a slave, Hagar has no rights. She may be pregnant with Abram's child, but she's still a second-class citizen. Sarai mistreats Hagar, causing the girl to run into the wilderness to escape the situation. And there in the desert, a powerful interaction takes place.

HE IS THE GOD WHO SEES AND HEARS

In verse 7, we find Hagar "near a spring . . . beside the road to Shur." Imagine the scene. She's pregnant and alone. She's exhausted. Maybe she sits and cries. It's a mess—a mess created by others, albeit made worse by her attitude. She's run from the problem of Sarai and Abram and travels toward the northeast border of Egypt. Since she's originally from Egypt, it's safe to assume she wants to run home, back to the land of her birth.

Now, the Hebrew word *Shur* means "wall," so named after a defensive feature (whether natural, created, or a combination of the two) that protected the Egyptians from invasion. Metaphorically and literally, Hagar is in a wilderness moment, about to hit a wall. As she tries to run back to her Egyptian past, she fails to understand her future awaits in Canaan with Sarai and Abram. There's no way through to her potential, and while the past might seem safe, known, and secure, it's an absolute dead end.

How many times have we wanted to run into the safety of the known past rather than forge forward into our future potential?

And so now Hagar has stopped in her misery and finds herself at the point of decision. In a place of refreshing, she encounters the angel of the Lord,[1] who asks her two important questions: "Where have you come from? and "Where are you going?" She responds, "I'm running away from my mistress Sarai" (16:8). In her mind she has no future, but little does she know she's right where she needs to be. The angel of the Lord tells her to go back, explaining that her child is to be called Ishmael (meaning "God hears"). In this exchange, Hagar discovers her child carries the same promise as given to Abram's descendants (16:9–12). A promised destiny grows within her that extends far beyond what her circumstances indicate.

Hagar has an "ah-ha" moment and knows beyond a doubt that the Lord has seen her. She says, "You are the God who sees me," (16:13) and the place becomes known as "Beer Lahai Roi," meaning, "well of the Living One who sees me." By a stream of running water, she encounters the One who is living waters. She is seen, known, and heard, and she discovers she's not alone.[2]

We can see this pattern of encounter and promise throughout Scripture,[3] and I guarantee the same pattern is in your life too. It's a pattern we can all learn to lean back into and trust. God sees us all, believer and pre-believer alike, and each and every one of us is His happy place. Akin to His heart of love and affection for Ethan, the hairdresser in my local salon, God delights as He looks upon us all. Indeed, He sees and hears—and thoroughly loves—every single human being. And as He gazes upon us, He invites us into encounters with Him so we can learn how He adores us. He sees, hears, and knows who we are and what we're destined for. We are all His happy place.

HE IS THE GOD WHO KNOWS

The idea that God knows us, aware of our foibles and flaws, and yet loves us still is a big one to grasp. How He knows and adores even those who think He has nothing good to offer. How He's not offended or bothered by anyone's negative view of Him. How He simply loves each and every person to Himself as He shows them what He's created them for. It's a concept beyond our full comprehension, and yet He does.

We can see this clearly in the life of Nathanael. Look at the first interaction Nathanael has with Jesus (John 1:44–51). It's clear that Jesus knows him well, stating that Nathanael is a man in whom there is no guile, meaning he's honest, authentic, even genuine. He's one in whom there is no deceit—"nothing false." Oddly, though, in return Nathanael is certain nothing good can come from Nazareth, the place of Jesus' birth. Ironically, it's through Jesus that God shows Nathanael He is the God who sees, hears, and *knows* him well. Through Jesus He shows that goodness can come from wherever God chooses. The interaction surprises Nathanael:

> When Jesus saw Nathanael approaching, he said of him, "Here truly is an Israelite in whom there is no deceit."
>
> "How do you know me?" Nathanael asked.
>
> Jesus answered, "I saw you while you were still under the fig tree before Philip called you."
>
> Then Nathanael declared, "Rabbi, you are the Son of God; you are the king of Israel."
>
> Jesus said, "You believe because I told you I saw you under the fig tree. You will see greater things than that." He then added, "Very truly I tell you, you will see 'heaven open, and the angels of God ascending and descending on' the Son of Man."
> (John 1:47–51)

Literally and figuratively, Jesus sees who and where Nathanael is, locating him in time, place, and motive. Knowing that Nathanael doubts anything good could come from Nazareth, Jesus still invites him into greater intimacy. He shares with him the wonderful future God has set before him. Much like Hagar and the hairdresser, Ethan, Nathanael is invited to leave behind his past doubts and step into a future of potential.

Even when we doubt God has something good coming toward us, He sees, hears, and knows us well. He's perturbed neither by our lack of faith nor by our lack of knowledge of who He truly is. He invites us to come, see, talk, and walk through him—"the door"—to eternal life (John 10:9 ESV).

Nathanael immediately recognizes that Jesus knew him prior to meeting him. There was so much more for Nathanael, in whom there was no guile—more than what he could ever see for himself. Much like Hagar, who saw no future for herself or her child, Nathanael's lack of understanding where the promise would emerge limited him. It took a word from God, but first God would reveal that He saw, heard, and *knew* Nathanael before opening him up to the truth of who He was. In revealing who Nathanael was, Jesus then freed him to step into his future. For as we know, Jesus came to give him an abundant life (John 10:10).

It's the same for us, just as it was for Ethan. Regardless of our doubt, good things—greater than we can imagine—are always coming our way. Into our future our promises will be born. We all carry the seed of hope. If we will only stop and look to see, God will meet us on whatever road, in whatever wilderness, we find ourselves. In that place we'll discover we've always been near the spring of living waters, the One who sees, hears, and knows us all. He will provide life in the places we least expect it to flow, and to our delight we'll discover that we are His happy place.

With Ethan, I had the privilege of being the conduit for our loving God. In my willingness to flow, this young man saw God for who He was. This God whom I knew, loved Ethan so much that He reached through me to release His streams of living, loving waters. This outward flow caused a permanent shift in Ethan's reality. Like Hagar and Nathanael, he turned back to his future promise, and as with Hagar and Nathanael, on that pathway lay the fullness of his destiny.

So let me tell you what happened next.

GOD IS GOOD STORY: HE DISCOVERED HE WAS SEEN, HEARD, KNOWN, AND LOVED

To conclude the *God Is Good Story* I started at the opening of this chapter, some months later I was back at that same hair salon with my son, Matthew, to have his hair cut. I was chatting with a young mom who needed encouragement when she was called away to have her hair washed. She invited me to join her so we could continue talking. The Holy Spirit was up to something good!

I felt God's prompt to offer this young woman prayer, so I shared how we can all hear from God and then started relaying my story about a young man with whom God had called me to share and pray. The man washing her hair listened intently, and then when I shared the vision of this young man dancing, he interrupted our conversation.

"That was me," he said.

Surprised, I looked at him, then realized he *was* the same person. Ethan was the same yet totally different. Unrecognizable. The sense of striving was gone. The style of dress, makeup, nail varnish, jewelry, and affected speech had disappeared. He'd clearly settled into who he was. Here before me stood a gentle, beautiful young man.

"You don't know the impact of that day," he told me. "I read what you gave me every morning. I showed it to everyone who would listen to me, and I still have it." He reached into his pocket, and from his wallet he pulled a worn, frayed piece of paper. Tape held it together along the seams where it had been folded many times.

He went on. "You don't know what this meant to me. What you did . . ." Apparently lost for words, he paused, then said, "*This* changed my life!" He shared how he'd felt loved and accepted that day and was so affected by what I said about the Father's love for him that he'd completely changed his life. The impact was clear to me in his demeanor and dress, but most significant for him was that he'd begun to pursue a childhood dream he'd previously felt unqualified to chase and had cast aside. But after that day, he felt worthy and enrolled in a creative writing course. Now he was writing science fiction novels, the dream that truly captured his heart.

I was delighted. Ethan was at peace, joy-filled, and at ease with himself. Gone was the young man whose attitude screamed *Accept me!* Instead stood a gentle, articulate person, his face shining with the promise of being loved and accepted.

THE POWER OF LOVE TO SAVE

I've since reflected that if I had addressed anything but the Father's heart for Ethan, I would have heaped more condemnation upon his shoulders. It was in the moment of the Holy Spirit's rebuke that I learned a powerful lesson. Being told a part of Ethan's life was none of my business, I recognized I am to release God's love and God will do the rest. God saw and knew Ethan better than me. After all, he was God's happy place.

I might know, see, sense, or understand the problems and issues a person (or even a church or a nation) has, but it's not for me to point them out and broadcast them. Rather, it's incumbent on me to release the Father's heart of love, His solutions, and grace.

Lesson learned! I was to always remember that God sees, God hears, God knows, and God loves us so much that He gave His only Son, not to condemn the world but to save it (John 3:16–17). So the questions to ask are these: What does that sort of love look like? What did the God who sees and hears say to Hagar? What did Jesus, who knew Nathanael, say to him?

For Ethan, love looked like acceptance. A father's delight in watching him be him. A father's blessing! The knowledge that God the Father saw him, heard him, and knew him released the grace for him to become who he truly was—a gentle young man.

I don't believe God worries about our or anyone's "issues" as much as we do. He has it (and them) in hand. He had Hagar and Nathanael in hand too. Rather, I believe God is more concerned that first people understand how thoroughly He adores them. How He sees, hears, and knows them. From a place of love and acceptance, people flourish and step into their futures. They need to learn of God's goodness and kindness first. Then from that place, they step into a relationship. The rest of the "stuff" is between God and them! In John 3:17 we read, "God did not send his Son into the world to condemn [or judge] the world, but to save the world through him."

In the original Greek, the word translated "save" is *sózó*. It means to save, but it also means to bring safely, to get well, to be made well (so "to heal"). It also means to preserve, to recover, to restore, to make whole. So Jesus came to deliver, protect, heal, preserve, do well for us, and make us whole. Now that sounds like a good God to me!

Love works out a multitude of issues. God knows what each person needs and when they need it. We release God's love—we strengthen, encourage, and comfort (1 Corinthians 14:3)—and the rest is a work for the Holy Spirit.

And so this young man who had read of God's love for him every morning since I'd stepped out to bless him felt accepted for the first time in his life. Ethan knew God adored and loved him. And in this place of being loved, he settled gently into pursuing his dream while allowing the other to drop away. He'd stepped into becoming fully himself—a restoration to his true self had begun.

Has Ethan accepted Jesus Christ as Lord and Savior? I don't know. But he tasted and saw God's goodness, and that was what God wanted for him at that moment. He understood that he was God's happy place. Ethan encountered Jesus Christ, the spring of living waters, and from that time he could trace the hand of a loving God in his life. Love and acceptance came from the very place of perceived rejection, from the place he least expected it to flow forth. It came from that place where he thought nothing good could ever come, and yet like Nathanael and Hagar, he discovered God saw, heard, and knew him. El Roi, "the God who sees," accepted and loved him, and that was what mattered most.

God is always present to us, but are we always present to Him? If we will stop and listen for what He'll say, we'll be surprised at how often He speaks to us throughout the day. When you find yourself in the wilderness, or even in the humdrum of everyday life, you'll discover that God sees, hears, and knows you too. And in that space you'll come to discover you are His happy place.

QUESTIONS TO CONTEMPLATE

1. How do you feel seen, heard, and known by God? What clues suggest He's always been by your side? How do these moments of awareness make you feel?
2. When have you run from moments of anguish in your past, and how did you seek and/or encounter God?
3. How has God placed great promise and destiny in those moments? What are those promises, and what have you learned from revisiting some of those times?

RESPONSE TO THE REVELATION

- **Action Step 1:** Each morning this week, ask God to show you moments throughout your day that demonstrate He sees, hears, and knows you. Then each evening, share with someone the goodness of God you saw in your life that day. Make this a habit, and you'll soon see God in everything you do and everywhere you go.
- **Action Step 2:** Ask God to highlight someone He would like you to stop for and offer prayer. If you miss the first one, ask for another chance. He is the God of second chances.

LET'S PRAY

Father, I ask that as You did with Hagar, Nathanael, and Ethan, help me perceive You as the God who sees, hears, and knows me. Help me recognize You, and guide me through my days. In Jesus' mighty name I pray, amen.

2

FEELING GOD'S ATTENTION

When the Lord saw that he had gone over to look, God called to him from within the bush, "Moses! Moses!" And Moses said, "Here I am."
Exodus 3:4

THE POWER of being seen by God is profound, and encountering Him radically changes us. We transform as we experience God's love, and in doing so we learn we are His happy place. As our hearts and minds renew, we begin to see God in a different way and start to feel His loving attention. Over the years, many have said to me, "How can I be certain God sees me? I want to have an encounter like that hairdresser. I want to feel God's attention too!"

My answer is inevitably the same: We can all feel God's attention for ourselves by intentionally looking for Him in everyday moments. It's celebrating God in the nuances and so-called coincidences throughout our days. We look for and choose to recognize those tiny moments that bring joy and say to ourselves, *Oh, there He is*. There's a whisper in the wind, the movement of trees. There's deep, unexplainable joy in moments of grief, or there's the phone call from a friend when we need encouragement or kindness the most.

These "coincidences" are interlaced with the fingerprints of heaven and release the fragrance of love throughout our lives. These moments may seem insignificant, but they're intentional kisses from God, who's saying, *I see you. I hear you. I know you. And I love you. Feel my attention, for I am here by your side.* If we choose to celebrate these small moments, we'll start to recognize God in them and feel His attention with greater ease. It's simply a matter of learning to turn aside to see.

GOD IS GOOD STORY: FEELING GOD'S ATTENTION THROUGH SEEING THE GOD WHO SEES

A while ago I felt sad, lonely, and misunderstood. My morning had been filled with supporting others from around the globe, and with my energy levels depleted, I felt defeated. To shake myself out of my low mood, I decided to go for a walk, calling to Matthew, my now teenage son, to come along since he was home for the day.

"Come on!" I called out. "We're going for a walk. Let's go get some lunch."

As we walked in the sunshine, I silently rebuked myself. *Pull yourself together and pull on your big girl boots. Come on. You know what to do. You train others in it. Don't merely talk the talk; walk the walk with integrity. Live as you preach and get your attitude sorted.*

We stopped for lunch at a local café, and as we sat at a table, I randomly looked at my phone. The time "1:11" flashed up on the screen.

I love you, I heard the Father whisper.

I love you too, I said back.

The time made me smile, for 1:11 is part of God's love language with me. For me, 1:11 refers to Mark 1:11, when at the baptism of Jesus, the voice of God, His Father, says, "You are My beloved Son, in whom I am well pleased" (Mark 1:11 NKJV). In this moment, God affirms Jesus for being Him—nothing more, nothing less. His identity revealed to all those around Him, God affirms His approval and love. It's important to catch the timing of this interaction between God the Father and Jesus the Son. It's before Jesus has done anything for

God. Here, God accepts, affirms, and loves His Son just for being Him.

So after years of seeing 1:11 everywhere, I recognize this as His whisper of love. And in those whispers I feel God's loving attention. They tell me I'm His beloved daughter, in whom He is well pleased. In fact, they tell me I'm His beloved daughter in whom He is well pleased and *delighted* (Mark 1:11 AMP). I am His happy place!

So returning to our story, with lunch finished, I went inside the café to pay the check and thought about an ARK (Act of Random Kindness) I'd performed in the same café a week earlier. I don't talk too much about these, and I wouldn't normally write about this one, but the goodness and kindness of God radiates by sharing what happened on this day. It's my hope you see Him in this story. It's my wish that you hear His heart. I trust it will encourage you to look for Him yourself, so you, too, can feel His attention throughout your day.

I had left a sum of money for ten or more coffees to be given away. Amazed and delighted, the girl behind the cash register said she'd never seen anything like it. She was excited by the idea. I laughed, telling her she would have fun choosing whom to bless. As we spoke, the café's atmosphere buzzed with the tangible presence of the Holy Spirit.

Now in my stinking thinking, I wondered why I'd bothered, noting an unpleasant exchange with the grouchy owner from a more recent visit when I'd merely tried to be friendly. I checked my attitude and chose to smile as I paid and left.

As we were walking home, quite some way down the street, we heard someone yelling behind us, "Excuse me! Excuse me!"

We stopped and turned to see the girl from the café running toward us, waving her arms.

"Excuse me," she said breathlessly as she caught up with us. Matthew and I waited for her to catch her breath, then she said, "You! You! You're the person who left the money at the register last week, aren't you?"

"Yes, that was me."

"You don't know what you did that day. It was amazing. You *broke* something open. I've never seen it before, but two more people came in that day and they left money for free coffees too."

"Wow. That *is* bizarre," I said.

I know people leave money in local cafés. It happens regularly at another café a suburb away from where I live. But she hurriedly explained that she'd never seen it happen in this café.

"I simply had to tell you," she went on. "I had to let you know. You started something, and others followed and did the same."

Now, what she didn't know was that she was inadvertently referencing my kingdom identity and life purpose. I've received repeated prophecies calling me a "breaker" and telling me I carry a "breaker anointing." Over the years I've seen things break open for those I walk with and coach. In this moment this young girl unknowingly affirmed my identity and purpose on a day I was struggling to see the reason behind it all.

A little embarrassed but close to tears, I smiled and thanked her for sharing the testimony with me.

In that 1:11 moment, God said to me, *I see you. I love you, and I accept you. You don't have to do a thing for me to love you any more than I already do. You are My beloved daughter, in whom I am well pleased. You are my happy place.* In this I felt His attention and complete love for me. Then with my core identity and value reestablished, God said through a young girl excited about ten free coffees and someone else doing it too, *I see you. I know you. This is who you are. You make a difference. You do matter. What you do affects and changes people for the better. Keep being you, keep doing what you are doing. Through you My love changes things!*

This picked me up immediately. I heard my Father's voice, but more importantly, He'd seen me in the moment I needed Him most. God knew my heart and thoughts, and He met me in my moment of need. He said, *My daughter, I love you,* and He did so even as I entertained thoughts of "poor me." I'd felt God's attention, and in the same way, you can too.

A BASIC HUMAN NEED

We all need to know God sees and cares for us no matter how long we've been walking with Jesus. And when that truth becomes an experienced reality, all bets are off! Feeling God's attentive gaze is life-changing as we learn to recognize we are seen, heard, and known by the loving creator of the universe. Knowing how much He adores us, we can take on the world!

When I first became a Christian, I exercised my faith by choosing to believe in God even when I had doubts. Reared in an atheist home, I occasionally struggled with my faith, and much like the epileptic's father in Mark 9:14–26, I would sometimes exclaim, *Lord, I believe; help me in my disbelief!* I then consciously chose to believe, exercising my free will to do so. But I would also lean back into my previous experiences with Him. In coming to faith, I had an encounter, and when I look back over my life, I can recognize many other times when I'd experienced Him too.

Through retrospection, I knew His attention had been on me. The issue was on my end. I hadn't recognized Him in the moment. As a new Christian, I had to learn to recognize when His attention was on me. I could then lean into those moments in times of doubt or despair. In doing so my heart and soul were nurtured. Like "doubting Thomas," I focused on the evidence before me to help me in my disbelief.

Those remembered moments have become times I tangibly recall God's attention on me. They are not always moments of all the goose bump feels we sometimes get, but rather the deep knowing that God was always there. Interestingly, we all need to be seen, known, and heard. It's hardwired into us as human beings. We need to be known by others,[1] and by extension, if we're truly honest, we all need to know we're known by God too. This fundamental need doesn't surprise God in the slightest. His original intent was for us all to be in a deep, reassuring relationship with Him. He wants us to feel His attentive gaze. If this were not so, why did Jesus come to reconcile us back to His Father?

The intimate interaction between God, Adam, and Eve in the

garden of Eden provides a glimpse of God's original intent. They freely walked and talked with God, coming to meet Him at the very sound (the "ruah" or wind) of His presence. They recognized and responded to the sound of His breath, the sound of His "voice." They knew God's heart was turned toward them, and they regularly felt His attentive love.

Then in Genesis 3:8, when they attempt to hide from God, we can infer their recognition of His presence. This is their first attempt to hide from Him, not understanding the pointlessness of their actions. They lacked the insight that they could not hide, for how could they when the very breath upon their lips comprised God's substance. It's a futile activity, and yet they try. They hide from God, denying themselves of feeling His attention. And to this day we attempt to hide from Him too.

Nobly, we all convince ourselves we don't need the affirmation of a loving Father, and so we declare boldly, "My faith doesn't require me to know His tangible love. I don't need to feel God's attention on me!"

Sadly, when we hide from God, we also hide from others created in His image. Both attempts to hide are futile exercises. We hide nothing from Him—we only hide ourselves from ourselves. We may effectively hide from others, but as we do, we're the ones who will ultimately pay the price. In trying to hide from God, we deny ourselves the One who breathes life into our being. His name is on our lips until our last breath, and every cell in our being is calling out to be seen. In our very essence, we need God's attentive gaze. We all ache to know God sees, hears, and knows us, and we need to see, hear, and know Him too. Why else do we perform for the accolades of others? It's a deep-seated need only satisfied by the attentive gaze of our God.

But this necessity goes further than merely needing to be seen and heard. We also need to know God knows us, that we matter and that our existence has meaning. Just as children need to feel their parents' attention, we need to feel God's attention. And so it's strange that so many of us downplay this need. Regardless of what we claim, the need remains, and so we seek attention from all areas but God. He's the one that matters, and He's the one who will always see us through His lens of love, for we are His happy place!

You might say, "Oh, God is much too busy with 'the important stuff' to care about little ole me!"

My reply is, "It's His very nature to care about you and the smallest details of your life. He knows the number of hairs on your head! If that isn't caring about the details, I don't know what is!"

MARRIAGE AS AN ANALOGY

Marriage is an analogy that proves helpful. Throughout Scripture we're called the bride of Christ, so it makes sense to consider a healthy marriage. Let's take a look.

To say throughout a marriage *I know my spouse loves me* but never experience that love in tangible ways suggests a dysfunctional relationship at best. All marriages require some meaningful connection. I doubt I would have made it beyond a few years if my marriage functioned purely on an intellectual level. Intuitively, we understand that a healthy marriage requires more. We need to feel our spouse's attention, whether through words of affirmation, quality time, encouragement, acts of service, receiving gifts, or physical touch.[2]

So, too, our relationship with God. It's not a lack of faith to desire this, rather it's how our faith grows. We encounter His love, we feel His attention, and as we do, we learn His ways so that in times of doubt we can lean back into those moments and know He's there. We know Him, therefore we can trust Him when all else fails.

Of course, most of us intellectually acknowledge that God sees, hears, and knows us, but we need experiential knowledge of this reality too. And we can gain this by learning to "look to see," and as we do we learn to feel His attention.

THE GOD WHO PAYS ATTENTION

Many passages in the Bible demonstrate how we can feel God's attention. The interaction between Hagar and God is just one of those. Let's turn back to Genesis 16.

In the moment when Hagar is at her most desperate, she receives a promise giving her a hope and a future. She recognizes that God has seen her. With His promise, she now understands what to do—return from whence she came. She continues by saying, "I have now seen the One who sees me" (verse 13). She feels God's attention and is strengthened for her journey back. In this exchange she learns more about Him. No doubt she'd heard about the One with whom Abram interacted, but now she knew Him for herself. She felt seen amid her mess, worry, and concern.

There was no judgment from Him for her part in the mess. He didn't chide her for being arrogant or for provoking Sarai. He just showed her that He saw and loved her. Her encounter with the Lord was an invitation for her to see Him with greater clarity. Indeed, she sees Him with such clarity that she names Him El Roi—meaning "the God who sees." Such is the impact of feeling God's attention. In apprehending His true nature, she is given the privilege of being the first to name God in the Scriptures—a lone woman, encountering God whose attention she felt as the One who always sees.

AN INVITATION TO SEE

In all times and seasons, no matter how we feel, God is always there. We can't escape Him even if we want to. David sums it up well in Psalm 139. Take a moment to allow the Scripture to penetrate your being.

Where can I go from your Spirit? Where can I flee from your presence? If I go up to the heavens, you are there; if I make my bed in the depths, you are there. If I rise on the wings of the dawn, if I settle on the far side of the sea, even there your hand will guide me, your right hand will hold me fast. (Psalm 139:7–10)

We are *always* with Him, and He *never* forgets us. We can't be unseen. God's gaze fastens upon us, and regardless of our behavior, His gaze is always one of love.

In learning to recognize and celebrate these moments of His loving attention, we grow deep in the assurance that He is ever present. It's in moments of so-called serendipity coincidence that we receive what I call *the kisses of God*. If we have eyes to see and ears to hear, He will reveal Himself to us in everyday life. If we look with intentionality, we learn how He sees, hears, and knows us well. In turn we learn that He will ever be *before* us and allow Himself to be known *by* us too. We always have His attention, for He is a very good, kind, and loving God.

But I hear you ask, "How do *I* feel His attention?"

Again, I reiterate, we look to see.

LOOKING TO SEE THE "KISSES OF GOD"

Let's cast our attention back to the Scripture we opened this chapter with and place it within its greater context:

Now Moses was tending the flock of Jethro his father-in-law, the priest of Midian, and he led the flock to the far side of the wilderness and came to Horeb, the mountain of God. There the angel of the LORD appeared to him in flames of fire from within a bush. Moses saw that though the bush was on fire it did not burn up. So Moses thought, "I will go over and see this strange sight—why the bush does not burn up." When the LORD saw that he had gone over to look, God called to him from within the bush, "Moses! Moses!" And Moses said, "Here I am." (Exodus 3:1–4)

In Exodus 3 Moses is at work. He's living his everyday life, tending the flock for his father-in-law, Jethro. His life in Egypt is far behind him, and he's traveled a great distance *through the wilderness*, to "the *far side* of the wilderness." Having crossed the desert, he finds himself in Horeb, which means "desolate place." Lean into the symbolism here. Moses travels "to the far side of the wilderness" [therefore, he has journeyed through the wilderness]. He finds himself in the "desolate place," which interestingly is also Mount Sinai, "the mountain of the Lord."[3] It is here in "the desolate place," at the "mountain of the Lord," that Moses encounters the angel of the Lord.[4] Seeing He has Moses' attention; the angel reveals Moses' life destiny and purpose. Moses has encountered the God of Hagar. He has seen and encounters the God who sees, and no doubt, he feels God's attention too.

Holding this in mind, I say to you, "You who have found yourself at the far side of the wilderness, have hope, take heart, for God is there, ready to speak when He sees you turn to see."

TURNING TO SEE GOD

The above passage of Scripture communicates intentionality. God uses a burning bush to draw Moses' attention. On seeing it, Moses notices something different—it catches his greater focus, because it doesn't burn up. In response, Moses stops, and goes over to look. His attention shifts from seeing the burning bush to looking *at* the burning bush. Moses chose to *really* look, with the purpose of seeing what was going on. Moses has a concentrated focus—he looks to see.

When we look to see we're actually looking with the purpose of really seeing what's going on. Scripture continues, "When the LORD saw that he had gone over to look, God called to him from within the bush, 'Moses! Moses!' And Moses said, 'Here I am'" (Exodus 3:4).

Are you catching this? When the Lord *saw* him look to see, he called to Moses. Other Bible translations say, "When the LORD saw that he had turned aside to look."[5] God speaks when He *sees Moses looking to see*. God has his attention and so He speaks.

Now, if we can learn to be like Moses and look to see, we'll recognize God's attention. We need to look to see, listen to hear, and open our hearts to know so when something catches our attention, we know to stop and listen for God's voice. Having caught our eyes, ears, and heart, God will lean in to speak, and in this moment we'll feel His gaze. We simply need to learn how to recognize those moments as we go about our day. If in these moments we will turn aside to see, then we *will* see Him as He truly is. And because of the good Father He is, His arms will be wide open to encircle us with His love. We'll feel His loving attention because His gaze is always upon us. We'll feel His delight and know beyond a doubt that we're His happy place.

We can all practice this looking-to-see so it becomes second nature. In my story about the café, I mentioned 1:11 and its meaning for me. This came from a series of seeing those numbers at pertinent moments as I went about my day. I saw the numbers with such regularity that I stopped to ask *What are You telling me, Lord? What are You saying? Is there a message You're trying to communicate?*

As I explored the meaning of these so-called coincidences, I learned God was speaking to me. And now when I notice these numbers, I *feel* His attention upon me. In these moments I know I'm His happy place. In these moments I stop, smile, and tell Him I love Him too. They are His kisses for me, to let me know He's there, caring for *me*. Those "kisses" are also available for you, because *you* are His happy place too!

In Exodus 3, Moses is quick enough to turn to see. He actively looks. Moses saw the burning bush, and when God *saw Him turning to see*, He spoke. We can encounter any of the Godhead this way. If we're aware of what's going on as we go about our day, we'll enjoy some profound times, because sometimes the words are significant. Other times they're simply "sweet nothings," murmuring to us of His love. We only need to be aware and open to feeling God's attention at any time, in any place. God will speak in mountain-top moments, *and* He'll speak as we go about the mundane. And like Moses, we can learn to be quick enough to turn to see.

So if you've found yourself on "the far side of the wilderness" like Moses, have hope and take heart—God is there ready to speak. Stop, listen, look to see, and you will *feel* His loving attention upon you. And even if you're not on the far side of the wilderness, He's still right there with you. He's ready to speak at all times, for His loving attention is always upon us. We just need to learn to recognize the moment and turn aside to see.

QUESTIONS TO CONTEMPLATE

1. What are some moments when you've felt God's attention?
2. Write down some of the language God uses with you to let you know He's focused on you. Like 1:11 for me, what is

some of the personal love language He uses to communicate with you?
3. Look for "God coincidences" over the next week and journal them, outlining how they make you feel His attention upon you.

RESPONSE TO THE REVELATION

- **Action Step 1:** Each morning this week, ask God to show you a burning bush moment sometime during the day. When you notice such a moment, stop, turn, and look to see what He will say to you. As you do, note your emotions. How do you feel when you notice His signposts? Then each evening, share with someone about the goodness of God you felt. Make this a habit, and you'll soon feel God's attention every day.
- **Action Step 2:** Ask God to highlight where you might perform an ARK (Act of Random Kindness) and then step in and release God's goodness. Note how the atmosphere shifts as you do. Does it become lighter? Did you feel a slight wind? Examine how it feels. How did the people respond? If you miss the first ARK prompting from God, ask for another chance. He's ever ready to pour His loving-kindness through you into the world so that others might feel His attention upon them too.

LET'S PRAY

Father, thank You for being with me throughout my nights and days. Thank You for showing Your delight in me and guiding my ways. Help me recognize the burning bush moments in my everyday life that I might stop to turn and see. And in those moments, help me feel Your attention upon me. In Jesus' mighty name I pray, amen.

3

GOD ENCOUNTERS ARE AN INVITATION TO MORE

*"Whoever drinks the water I give them will never thirst.
Indeed, the water I give them will become in them
a spring of water welling up to eternal life."*
John 4:13–14

I HOPE you're catching the truth that encounters with God are available to you during your everyday life. Regardless of where you are or the mess you believe you're in, God is there, speaking to you and loving on you. His voice can be heard upon the wind or in conversations we have throughout our day. We hear Him within a friend's encouragement, and we'll encounter Him in unusual or so-called coincidental circumstances. His voice is the sound of many rushing waters (Revelation 1:15; Ezekiel 43:2). Even the lyrics of a song might resonate with what He wants to say. It's simply learning to recognize Him in our day.

These moments are how we can learn to feel God's attention. It's His delight to speak, and it's our delight to hear and respond, understanding that every encounter with God is an invitation to more. *But more of what?* you might ask. The "more" is more of God, a deeper understanding of who He is, a greater appreciation of His love. And woven through it all is a more thorough appreciation of who we're destined to become.

Moses was going about his day when he saw the burning bush and decided to have a look. Seeing He had Moses' attention, God spoke, and with that encounter unfolded a lifelong journey to "more" for Moses. We, too, can incline our ear to hear, our eyes to see, and our heart to know the God who speaks. Each encounter is a doorway through which we can engage our heart with a God who adores us and is ready and eager to show us the "more" He has for us, our families, our communities, and even our cities, regions, and nations.

GOD IS GOOD STORY: MY JOURNEY TO RECOGNIZING GOD'S INVITATION TO "MORE"

My journey toward recognizing Jesus Christ as my Lord and Savior is traceable back to when I was four or five years old. Born into an atheist (at best agnostic) family, I sought answers to questions beyond my age. I have a distinct memory of practicing the violin as a little girl and suddenly pondering death and what might happen thereafter. Brought up in a home that encouraged questions, I put down my violin and sought answers from my father. Who else would I go to? After all, he was the fountain of truth in my little world. He alone held the wisdom my childish heart yearned for, and as he had committed his life to ponder life's challenging mysteries, I felt certain he would know.

Walking into the kitchen I asked, "Dad, what happens when we die?"

He looked at me with all seriousness and simply said, "Your body dies, you're buried, and the worms eat you. You no longer exist."

Looking back, I realize that was a brutal answer. But in all my innocence I simply pondered further and decided it couldn't be true. What, or rather, *who* led me to this deliberation? What, or rather *who*, helped me decide it wasn't true? In this moment, I believe I encountered the living God. He led me to reject my father's insight; I *knew* my father was wrong. It was in this "knowing" that I heard God speaking to my childlike heart. It would take some time before I recognized His voice and His presence in my life, but each such encounter was always an invitation to know Him more.

At nine years of age, I asked a Catholic friend if I could pray to God and cross myself as they did in her home. She said she would need to first check with her mother. The following day she told me I had a green light, and so each night I prayed, asking God to care for my family, those I loved, the hungry, the orphaned, and the poor. In these nighttime prayers I can see the hand of God, but I still hadn't formally met the One my heart sought. It would be many more years before someone would point the way to lead me home.

At twelve years of age, in my first year of high school, the Gideons gave me a Bible. I tried to read it many times on my own but to no avail. I felt it held the key, but how or in what way I didn't know. Over the years I even asked various people to take me to church. I attended services of differing expressions of the Christian faith, yet no one showed me the way.

In each remembered moment of my journey I now recognize that the Holy Spirit was inviting me into more. I can look back and identify many pivotal moments, including a clear memory of, again, playing the violin. I was a teenager, and I felt something (or someone) enter into my room. It came with a sense of overwhelming love and caused tears as I felt what I now know was God's gentle kindness, peace, and deep joy. I naively thought the music had moved me, so I tried playing the piece again. But no matter how earnestly I tried, I could not muster the feeling. I now know I had encountered the one who is Love. The Holy Spirit was wooing me to Jesus. The encounter again was an invitation to something more. Sadly, what I needed was someone to lead me to Him, to explain who Jesus was, but no one was there to answer my heart's call. I was looking in the right places, but no one guided me through the Door.

I was nineteen years old when my father received a cancer diagnosis. Not long after, I attended a church service where a well-known biker preacher named John Smith (of the God Squad) spoke. Deeply moved, I went forward to the altar wanting prayer for my father and sobbed as I kneeled. It was a moment I can now describe as a divine invitation to encounter more of God, and yet not a soul in that church asked me if I knew Jesus. Instead, I kneeled with a stranger at the altar and asked God to heal my father. While the invitation to something more was open, I needed help in finding my way so I could encounter more.

And so with many more pivotal moments, my search continued until, at twenty-three, I came face-to-face with Jesus and said, with passion, "Yes, I do, yes I do, yes I do!"

People may think I'm mad looking for God in everything I do, but I know He always has more available, and I don't want to miss a thing. I've been called hyper-religious and even New Age because I see Him throughout my days, but with every encounter, there's always more of Him to explore. It's an endless journey with Him. I'm excited to encounter Him, and I understand that with each encounter He's inviting me into something greater, a deeper appreciation of who He is. And with that insight comes a better understanding of who I am too. He is with me in everything I do. I can encounter God in the same way I "encounter" a friend when I have a cuppa with them. Sometimes the encounter is life-changing, and other times we're simply doing life together.

And always remember, if we've given our lives to Jesus Christ, we've already had at least one encounter with God. However, with that encounter there's always an invitation to more. Whether or not there was an emotional response at the point of commitment, there *was* an encounter with the living God, for "no one can say, 'Jesus is Lord,' except by the Holy Spirit" (1 Corinthians 12:3). He saw you, you saw Him, and you stepped in. This pivotal encounter is merely the beginning. With each new encounter comes an invitation to see God anew. With each new encounter comes an invitation to explore and encounter more. God delights in us as we discover more about Him and more about ourselves. Never forget, we are His happy place.

AN ENCOUNTER WITH JESUS IS ALWAYS AN INVITATION TO ENCOUNTER MORE

The story of the woman at the well in John 4 is a beautiful example of how an encounter with God becomes an invitation to encounter so much more. One drink of His goodness leads to an eternal river of goodness flowing to us, within us, and through us.

In this story, Jesus is traveling through Samaria when He stops at Jacob's well (the place of encounter for Jacob in Genesis 28). As He rests there at noon, a woman comes to draw water. Her encounter with Jesus becomes an invitation where she's not only seen, heard, and known but offered more: "Jesus said to her, 'Will you give me a drink?' (His disciples had gone into the town to buy food.) The Samaritan woman said to him, 'You are a Jew and I am a Samaritan woman. How can you ask me for a drink?'" (John 4:7–9).

Let me highlight a few things for you. It's important to recognize that it was unusual for a Jewish person to speak with or even acknowledge her. Custom dictated that Jesus should completely ignore her. He was a man, in the presence of an unaccompanied woman. Further, she was a Samaritan. Samaritans, seen as pagans, were despised by the Jewish people, and their two communities clashed based on not just religion but race, culture, and even politics. And last—as we see next—this was a woman of questionable reputation. Yet Jesus speaks to her, and in speaking to her first He invites her to engage. In this act alone, He's acknowledging her existence and giving her worth.

The passage continues:

> Jesus answered her, "If you knew the gift of God and who it is that asks you for a drink, you would have asked him and he would have given you living water."
>
> "Sir," the woman said, "you have nothing to draw with and the well is deep. Where can you get this living water? Are you greater than our father Jacob, who gave us the well and drank from it himself, as did also his sons and his livestock?"
>
> Jesus answered, "Everyone who drinks this water will be

thirsty again, but whoever drinks the water I give them will never thirst. Indeed, the water I give them will become in them a spring of water welling up to eternal life." (John 4:10–14)

Here is the first invitation to "more," but before discussing it, let's read on:

The woman said to him, "Sir, give me this water so that I won't get thirsty and have to keep coming here to draw water."
He told her, "Go, call your husband and come back."
"I have no husband," she replied.
Jesus said to her, "You are right when you say you have no husband. The fact is, you have had five husbands, and the man you now have is not your husband. What you have just said is quite true."
"Sir," the woman said, "I can see that you are a prophet. Our ancestors worshiped on this mountain, but you Jews claim that the place where we must worship is in Jerusalem."
"Woman," Jesus replied, "believe me, a time is coming when you will worship the Father neither on this mountain nor in Jerusalem. You Samaritans worship what you do not know; we worship what we do know, for salvation is from the Jews. Yet a time is coming and has now come when the true worshipers will worship the Father in the Spirit and in truth, for they are the kind of worshipers the Father seeks. God is spirit, and his worshipers must worship in the Spirit and in truth."
The woman said, "I know that Messiah" (called Christ) "is coming. When he comes, he will explain everything to us."
Then Jesus declared, "I, the one speaking to you—I am he." (John 4:15–26).

When I think of this exchange, I see the woman as a little startled. She's out at noon, which is a strange time to collect water since water collection was usually done in the cool of the day. Given the time, she's presumably hiding in shame. No doubt she's been rejected by the people of her town due to her living arrangements, and therefore avoiding all interaction if possible, when a Jewish man (symbolic of all the men who had rejected her in the past) speaks to her.

She must be thinking, *Who is this guy? He's talking to me, asking me for a drink, and then saying I should ask him for a drink instead!* Understandably, she completely misses the point. Imagine her relief when she's told she won't have to come out to draw water from this well anymore. *If he can give me everlasting waters, I can retreat and never expose myself to ridicule and shame again.* Little does she realize she stands completely exposed, for Jesus sees right through her.

We can assume this woman at the well—historically known in some church traditions as Photini (meaning "luminous one" or "enlightened one")—suffered many past rejections. In her day, divorces could be obtained only by men, and they could be granted for the most trivial of reasons. Men held all the power in marital relationships, so by inference, Photini was repeatedly rejected by the ones who should have been protecting her.

It's a life-changing interaction for Photini. In speaking first, Jesus draws her in and then immediately identifies her greatest perceived need—a never-ending water supply so she never needs to return to the well at noon again. Imagine her shock when He speaks, acknowledging her existence, asking *her* for something and then offering her a solution to her plight. He says He can satisfy all thirst. In surprise, she points out the impossibility of the matter—He has nothing to draw water with. But then she immediately says, "Yes, please!" It's a brave move to even respond to Him, but can you see her being drawn in? He offers a salve for her pain, a solution to her woes, ever-flowing water without exposure to others.

Of course, Jesus isn't done. He draws her out further, and in doing so highlights that she has no husband. With a word of knowledge He clarifies He truly sees her, and yet His invitation stands. Regardless of her past or what she or others might think, He demonstrates complete acceptance. I imagine her deep in disappointment at this stage. Her past has caught her out, but at least she owns the moment and admits she has no husband. Think how her heart must have sunk.

There is no hiding. Jesus fully exposes her pain, and in all her rejection she does what any of us might do: She deflects the conversation from herself. She tries to shift the focus to politics and religion instead, for these are far-safer topics to discuss with this lone man she encounters than her lack of marital bliss. Not allowing anyone too close, she functions as a woman, shamed by a life she never desired, cast aside by those who should have loved her as she avoids all those who might shame her further.

Jesus acknowledges her deflection, addresses the religious and political arguments, clarifies what true worship looks like, and invites again. He gently brings the conversation back to the answer her heart is longing for, yet she'd never known it did. Nonetheless, she wants to be seen in her mess and accepted. And so He's letting her know this: *There is so much more than what you understand or what you perceive. What God truly desires is people who worship in spirit and in truth, because it's the heart that really matters, and you, too, qualify.*

Jesus reveals God's desire for people of the heart and shows that politics and religious arguments are not important. It's always been about the heart, and with that, He declares He is the awaited-for Messiah, the one called Christ. He simply says, "I am he" (John 4:26).

AN ENCOUNTER POINTS BACK TO GOD'S NATURE

Let's reflect on Jesus' declaration, "I am he." He's revealing to her (a woman, no less!) His identity as the awaited-for Messiah. Now think back to Moses' exchange with God at the burning bush. God tells Moses "I Am Who I Am" (Exodus 3:14). Can you see the similarity?

Now reflect on the power contained within the same statement when said to the crowd in the garden of Gethsemane. Upon going out to meet them, Jesus asked:

"Who are you looking for?"
"Jesus of Nazareth," they replied. (Now Judas, the traitor, was among them.)
He replied, "I am he."

And the moment Jesus spoke the words, "I am he," the mob fell backward to the ground! (John 18:4–6 TPT)

I think the revelation of Jesus' true identity contained such power that it caused Photini to leave her jar and run straight back to the very people who had rejected her. What must she have been feeling to cause her to do that? Her encounter with Jesus contained an invitation to know Him more, and in that moment of revelation came an even deeper recognition of His acceptance of her. Seeing her in all her mess, He calls her to come just as she is. He is the Messiah who sees her, and He sees deep into her soul. Inviting her to encounter more, to receive endless living waters, He shares that He is the one "waited for," and she is invited in.

The outcast, the Samaritan, the one living in adultery—none of it mattered. Jesus was inviting her to so much more, because she was His happy place! This was no mere invitation to simply drink from a bucket at noon when no one else was around. It was a profound invitation to drink from a flowing river of life. This river became a flow so great that she couldn't contain it. Transformed in an instant, she becomes "Photini" and runs back into the very community that had rejected her and exclaims, "Come, see a man who told me everything I ever did. Could this be the Messiah?" (John 4:28–29). Upon hearing and seeing her, they respond in such a way that we can only marvel at the extreme transformation that must have occurred in Photini.

Like Hagar and Moses in the desert, Nathanael, and my hairdresser, too, this woman was seen by Jesus. But more importantly, He let her know that He saw her.

The invitation Jesus gave her is the same for us all: *If you come to Me, you will have living waters that will rise up from the inside of you, and you—rejected and cast aside one—will affect a nation. There is so much more, more than you can imagine or see!* And impact a nation this Samaritan woman did, and affect a nation you can too!

Her story continues:

> Many of the Samaritans from that town believed in him *because* of the woman's testimony, "He told me everything I ever did." So when the Samaritans came to him, they urged him to stay with them, and he stayed two days. And because of *his* words many more became believers.
>
> They said to the woman, "We no longer believe just because of what you said; *now we have heard for ourselves, and we know that this man really is the Savior of the world.*" (John 4:39–42, emphasis added)

WE RECEIVE MORE AND WE FLOW

This despised woman—lonely, cast aside from society, and hiding—is the first recorded to witness Jesus Christ as Messiah. Her response? She *runs* to share the good news, plowing the ground where Philip the evangelist reportedly comes later to preach and perform miracles. She's the forerunner, the "breaker" for what is to come. As she—a woman—is elevated to leadership, Jesus shows her worth to all. Through His treatment, He demonstrates Photini's value, and through the impact of her life, He affirms not only who she is but *whose* she is, for she was *His* happy place!

I love how fully restored she is. Like Hagar, she runs back into her place of pain. Receiving the living waters of Jesus Christ, she's made clean, set free to be fully alive to Him, no less herself yet *more fully* herself. A despised and ignored woman seen by Jesus receives more than just an encounter *with* Jesus; she receives her purpose—a hope and a future—because He saw her and called her into how truly remarkable she was. She shone with His acceptance and love.

This woman's transformation drew people to Jesus. Because of her testimony, they came and saw, experiencing Jesus for themselves. There was more available to her and more for those she invited. Her community no longer believed through the power of her testimony but through their own testimony as well. They encountered Jesus for themselves, and in their encounter was an invitation to so much more!

So, too, we draw the world to Jesus through our experiences of and with Him. From the "more" of Him, we overflow and invite others into our more by providing a drink to those willing. Then from there, many will learn to drink for themselves. It is simple, it is beautiful, and it is profound!

If we will take time to turn aside to see the One who is living waters, He will meet us where we are. Throughout our days, He will become our drinking well, and we can draw deep from Him, for He never runs dry—there is always more. We will also have enough left over for others, because there's surplus when Jesus is in our midst.[1] He whispers to us, *You no longer need to draw water for yourself in your own strength. Let Me become a flowing river of life to you, through you, and from you to others. Let us together become an encounter that encapsulates an invitation to more of Me.*

Jesus will do this for us all, regardless of who we think we are or what we think we've done. We don't perform for His love but flow forth from His love. He will refresh us so we feel seen, accepted, and adored. He will flow with such abundance that we won't be able to contain Him to ourselves. The "more and more and more" of God will cause us to overflow with His goodness. He sees right through us as His waters of life wash away all pretense and hiddenness, causing us to become more fully who we are as we allow Him to be more fully Himself with us, in us, and through us.

It truly is a matter of "We love because he first loved us" (1 John 4:19). He is there, waiting to encounter us all.

ACCESSING THE LIVING WATERS AS WE GO

You may be wondering, *How do I access these living waters? Can I encounter Jesus such that I shine as a luminous one too? Can I have more?*

My answer is, "Yes, of course you can!" Jesus will always meet us in our place of need, but He also promises that if we seek Him, He will come (Matthew 7:7–8). Either way, as we partake, we will shine. Remember, if we've given our lives to Jesus Christ, we've already had an encounter with God. Whether or not we know it, the mere act of saying yes means the Holy Spirit has encountered us and invited us to step through Jesus, the Door. Even one encounter with Jesus Christ is an invitation to taste and see the endless living waters that He is. He came that we might have life and have it to the full (John 10:10). He came to give us an abundant life, overflowing with so much more!

For this woman at the well there was an invitation to more than she could ever hope or dream. So, too, for us.

In every moment of encounter, we are invited to more. And we'll encounter more of Him "at the well"—when dropping the children off at school, while taking out the garbage, in worship, at work, or in a store. In the mundane everyday moments God will speak to us. He'll catch our attention in our daily lives. If we stop and look to see what He will say to us, He will speak. I believe these are the moments that contain within them an invitation to so much more. He says, *I see you, I love you, and you need do nothing more than be fully who you are, for I will never love you any less. Nor could I love you any more than I already do.*

We must learn to look for the invitations. We must learn to taste and see that He is good. As you look, you will see, and whatever you focus on will grow. What you delight in becomes more apparent. And there is the promise that if you delight yourself in the Lord, He will give you the desires of your heart (Psalm 37:4). If your heart's desire is Him, then you will certainly receive the abundance available. You will step into a delight inconceivable as He gives Himself to you more and more and more.

An encounter at the well, wherever you may be, is really an invitation to partake of the living waters. We then take those waters out to the streets, the towns, the cities, and the nations. We take Jesus with us into the neighborhoods, the office blocks, the schools, and the stores. Wherever you live, wherever you go, you take Him with you. But first you must learn to drink so you can provide a drink for others, for that is where there's always more. Eventually, you learn to constantly draw on the tap that never runs dry.

So let's learn to look, taste, see, focus, and delight in Jesus, and in this way we will encounter all God has for us. For in every encounter there's always an invitation to more.

QUESTIONS TO CONTEMPLATE

1. When was a time that you, others, or circumstances in your life caused you to want to retreat and hide? What does Jesus have to say about those circumstances? Ask Jesus where He was in those circumstances, how He saw you then, and how He sees you now. Journal your answers.
2. Have you ever had a season when telling others about Jesus was easy and you flowed freely with His love? When was that, and what was it like? If you stopped flowing, what caused you to stop? Chat with God about your thoughts and journal what He says to you.
3. Think about an encounter with God the Father, Jesus, or the Holy Spirit. Then to the best of your ability, recall all the details of that encounter. As you do, ask God to reveal more about it. Are there details you missed? Is there a deeper place you can go? Ask God if there's more. Then journal what you experience, see, and hear.

RESPONSE TO THE REVELATION

- **Action Step 1:** Each day this week, create some quiet time when you can read John 4. As you do, imagine yourself at the well and ask Jesus to give you a drink of His living waters. Ideally, do this in the morning, but any time of day is great. In your imagination, see yourself with Him, receiving a drink and drinking it. Note how it makes you feel. Make this a habit, and you'll soon feel refreshed in ways you never thought possible.
- **Action Step 2:** Ask God to highlight where He would like you to flow with His living waters. Who can you stop for

and offer prayer? Who can you call, email, or message and release an encouraging word? Let God know you're ready and willing to refresh others and want His living waters to not only flow to you but through you.

LET'S PRAY

Father God, thank You for the gift of Jesus Christ inviting me always into more of You. Help me become aware of the endless flow of Your living waters in my life that I might return to a place of refreshing and discover yet more. Help me see You in ways I've not seen You before, and help me seek more of You so I might have more. Help me encounter You and see You afresh, and with a deeper revelation of You, help me discover more. And when I do, God, help me flow freely with Your goodness to others that they may, too, discover Your loving-kindness and that there is always more of You. In Jesus' mighty name I pray, amen.

4

THE COMMAND TO BE STILL

Be still, and know that I am God.
Psalm 46:10

AN ENCOUNTER WITH JESUS, the living waters, will change you forever. Never the same, you'll have a hankering for more. Drawn to the One who embodies love, our story of encounter will draw others to Him so they may encounter Him for themselves. Each encounter with God contains an invitation to explore who He is with greater depth.

To see and encounter God in our daily lives is normal Christianity. God is everywhere and always with us. We can recognize His fingerprints through an active, intentional looking-to-see as we go about our day. As we grow in this habit, we'll see Him in everything, in everyday moments, speaking, encouraging, caring, and loving. We develop a language of love and an ability to recognize Him as He nurtures us to the core of our being. It's a beautiful, active way of doing life with God. He is ever present with us as an ever-caring Father, watching and guiding us all.

Beside this active looking is another way we can look to see God. It, too, is an intentional positioning, but it's not as we go about our usual everyday living. Rather, it comes through setting aside time where we learn to be still *with* God. He often yearns for us to simply be still and know that He is God. If we position ourselves to hear what He'll say to us in quiet moments, we'll be astounded at the depths of the love He has for us.

THE INVITATION IS CAST—BEING STILL WITH GOD

Throughout Scripture we can find encouragement to set aside time to be still with God. A favorite verse of mine is Psalm 46:10, where God explicitly encourages us to "be still, and know that [He is] God."

The practice of stillness is as old as time itself, and it's all about where we choose to gaze. Choice is a powerful tool for catching "God moments." Choosing to look to see throughout our day, choosing to see in the quiet moments we set aside—both are important and create a richness in our lives. Our ability to choose where we gaze, to choose what we focus on, is profound. To set aside time to be still with God honors Him and acknowledges the price Jesus paid. God values our freedom to choose so much that He died for us (and as us) to maintain our freedom to choose Him or not. So choosing stillness to know Him speaks volumes about who He is to us. Rather than force us into a relationship with Him, He asks us to choose Him. It's not only in the moment of salvation that we "pick Jesus," but in our response to choose to spend time with Him in stillness over all the other things we could do with our time. We honor the sacrifice He made by choosing to be still as we spend time to seek Him, see Him, and *be* with Him. We choose Him (or not) over and over again as we decide what to do with our time.

An invitation to consciously be with God is always there, but to truly *be* with Him requires us to quiet ourselves in a place of stillness. There we will hear Him well. It's in that place of hearing that we come to know Him better. If we choose to accept the invitation, our time spent with Him will bring dividends. I can assure you there will always be something fighting for your time, but as we exercise our choice through where we spend it and in that time set our sights on the Father, we bring great delight to His heart.

But regardless of what we choose, we remain His happy place.

LEARNING TO BE STILL

God extends an ever-present invitation to see Him face-to-face. The invitation has always been there, and He gives it to all humankind regardless of race, creed, gender, age, or social status. He whose name we could not speak made access to us *all* through the Door, Jesus Christ.

Jesus affirms the invitation is always at hand. He says, "I am the door. If anyone enters by me, he will be saved and will go in and out and find pasture" (John 10:9 ESV).

We choose to spend the time. *We* choose to enter. But we must remember that this concept of "entering a door" is merely a metaphor, because how can we enter a place in which we inhabit. Similarly is the concept of ascension. Please recognize how we adopt these turns of phrase to help us conceptualize becoming present to God, when in truth we are always present. Scripture reveals we are in Him and with Him, and if we have accepted Him as Lord and Savior, He is always within us. There is no place we can go to escape Him (Psalm 139:7). Language serves to assist our awareness of this truth, and metaphor is merely the vehicle through which that truth communicates.

So we can see God in our lives amid the busyness, and we can see Him in the quiet times too. As with any relationship, it's a process of recognition, a turning to see, an acknowledgment, regardless of where we are or what we're doing. Eventually, we catch the truth that "being still" is possible even amid our busyness. It becomes a state of our hearts. However, to learn how to host this reality, and for the ease of this journey, I suggest being still is an act of will where we quiet ourselves and spend time with God. It's a dedicated time set aside, much like we might have a date night with a spouse or a coffee catch-up with a friend. This type of quality time helps us learn how to recognize His voice and see His fingerprints through our life. It also allows time for us to breathe, not so much for His sake, although He loves being with us, but more for our sake. It is *for us* that He draws us to

Himself. In this space, He restores our soul, whispers sweet nothings, and calls out our kingdom name and purpose.

This is a mystery of grand proportions. To be still and know that He is God—to *know* Him intimately, experientially—is too marvelous to even contemplate, and yet we must. Having grown up outside the Christian faith, this still astounds me. The mere concept that I could have a cup of tea with the creator of the universe, that He would even care, speaks volumes about who He is. The way to know God in this intimate and beautiful way is through learning to abide. It is simply learning to be still, and from there we grow to know.

TO BE STILL AND KNOW—WHEN SAMUEL LAY DOWN

To understand this mystery a little more, let's look to Samuel the prophet. Committed to the Lord before conception by his mother, Samuel ministers to the Lord under the guidance of Eli. In taking up the story at 1 Samuel 3, we find the young Samuel eager to please his mentor. We read how Eli's eyesight has grown dim, and how, sadly, his leadership of his own sons lacked integrity and wisdom. So perhaps Eli's eyesight had grown dim not only in the natural but in the spirit, too, which perhaps accounts for his delayed recognition of what's occurring to Samuel:

> In those days the word of the LORD was rare; there were not many visions. One night Eli, whose eyes were becoming so weak that he could barely see, was lying down in his usual place. The lamp of God had not yet gone out, and *Samuel was lying down in the house of the Lord, where the ark of God was.* (1 Samuel 3:1–2, emphasis added)

The Scripture continues to explain how God calls to Samuel three times, and each time the boy runs to Eli saying, "Here I am; you called me" (3:5–8).

In this passage you'll see that Samuel isn't familiar with the voice of the Lord and hasn't yet learned to recognize the sound of His voice.

And so because he was yet to grow in this ability, Samuel mistakenly thinks his master Eli is calling him. Samuel goes to him a few times before Eli realizes what's happening. After the third time that Samuel comes to him, Eli recognizes the Lord is calling the young boy.

Oh, that we would all have someone to guide us this way! Eli tells Samuel, "Go and lie down, and if he calls you, say, 'Speak, Lord, for your servant is listening'" (3:8–9).

We witness the patience of God, calling each time to Samuel, while allowing him (with Eli's help) to work it out. In verse 19 we read how "the Lord was *with* Samuel as he grew up" (emphasis added), just as He's with us all today. And as Samuel positions himself in the Presence (in the temple of the Lord), he grows in *knowing* God. Eventually Samuel becomes so acquainted with the Lord's voice that God "let none of Samuel's words fall to the ground" (v. 19).

Look how Eli encourages Samuel to position himself to hear God. He encourages the boy to return to where he was when the call first occurred. This positioning to hear is what being still and knowing God is all about. Samuel does as Eli says, and when he hears the voice again, *this time* he knows what to do. Positioned to hear, Samuel looks to see, listens to hear, and readies himself to know what the Lord will say in this moment.

WE ARE LIVING TEMPLES IN A BETTER COVENANT

Like Samuel, we can all position ourselves to recognize and respond to the voice of the Lord. Remember, we are a people of a better covenant than the one Samuel was under (Hebrews 8:6). We have free access to God through Jesus Christ. The crucifixion of Jesus removes the division between us and God. We all have access to the living God, and those who accept Jesus Christ as Lord and Savior are temples of the living God. Therefore, when we lie down to spend time with Him, we position ourselves just as Samuel did, with immediate access to the temple of God. We are in Him, and He is in us. Wherever we are, God is. It just requires a little quiet time, focus, and trust.

I guarantee we can all encounter Him, and I dare say we not only *can* encounter Him but *will* encounter Him. It's just a matter of being still and then learning how to recognize His voice. We will see, hear, and know Him. He will see that we do, because He's far keener for us to recognize His voice than we are to learn how to recognize it. As for Samuel, it's just a matter of learning to recognize it's God when He speaks and responding as He does.

LOOKING TO SEE AND LISTENING TO HEAR

The idea of being still before the Lord, of waiting for Him to speak, is found throughout the Scriptures. One of my favorite passages is in Habakkuk 2. Habakkuk comes before the Lord with an agenda, but it's essentially the same concept of waiting upon the Lord. Habakkuk outlines a complaint and makes a demand on Him. However, even though he's coming with an agenda, this example shows how we can intentionally position ourselves to see what God might say to us. Like Samuel, Habakkuk is positioning himself to hear from the Lord: "I will stand at my watch and station myself on the ramparts [protective barriers]; I will look to see what he will say to me, and what answer I am to give to this complaint" (Habakkuk 2:1).

See the active expectation in Habakkuk's looking? It's not a looking to see as he goes about his day, but a *being still* "on the ramparts." *He is waiting, in anticipation, for God to speak.*

Like Habakkuk, we can look to see, and like Samuel, we can position ourselves and listen to hear. We can all spend time waiting upon the Lord to hear the voice of God. Samuel waited with no agenda. Habakkuk stilled himself for an answer after outlining a complaint. Both are examples of being still to know and are legitimate ways of interacting with God.

BEING STILL IN THE RUSH OF LIFE

Being still in the rush of life is the most effective way to learn how we can encounter God, who is never absent from our lives. The being still I'm referencing is not *doing* anything in particular. Stillness can include many activities, or none. It requires a positioning of the heart, a quieting of our inner selves, our thoughts, and our surroundings and looking to see what God might say.

It helps to start with being physically still. We lie down or sit down as we quiet our inner thoughts. When we allocate this type of time with God, He will be there. He may or may not speak. We might receive answers to questions—solutions to problems. We might receive brilliant ideas. Or we might feel nothing. Regardless, we will *always* be refreshed. Whatever happens, we never waste time when we spend it with God.

GOD IS GOOD STORY—GIVE ME AN HOUR. IT WILL BE WORTH YOUR TIME.

A few years into my practicing being still with God, He said, *Give me an hour. It will be worth your time.*

It was the last week of school term in a very busy week. My daughter was changing schools, and I was running ragged taking care of everything such a change entailed. We were hosting a birthday party for said daughter and preparing to go away on the weekend. The pressure was on to complete a mountain load of tasks with limited time and energy.

In the middle of this week, late one evening my daughter announced she'd lost her retainer. To replace it was going to cost time and money—$450, to be exact. So we looked everywhere we could. We searched the plausible places, and in desperation, we searched the implausible ones too. We turned out the dog bed and, with the aid of a flashlight, scoured the school playgrounds, including all the trash cans. Then we searched the house again, praying the retainer would miraculously show.

It didn't, so I made the necessary appointments with the orthodontist.

The day of the appointment was frantic. I dropped my four-year-old son at kindergarten, and with only one and a half hours to complete my many jobs, I felt rushed. I then had to turn around, collect my daughter, race to get my son, and get my daughter to the appointment. I was bone weary, and as I drove home from dropping my little one off, I could feel God calling me to spend time with Him.

Feeling irritated, I responded, *But I have so much to do. I must collect Rebekah early, get her to the orthodontist, get her to an eye appointment, and do all the shopping ready for the last day of school. Her birthday is in two days, and I must prepare for that too. I simply don't have time.*

For those who are shocked by what I just shared, please know you can be real with God. You can talk to Him like that. He knows you feel the way you do anyway, and as a loving Father He wants to have an authentic conversation with you. So let's just be honest with Him and express how we feel.

Now, regardless of how real you can be, I felt bad that I'd responded in such a way. I hadn't been well for some time, and I was finding it difficult to cope with all I had on my plate. On the cusp of chronic fatigue, I was in a state of complete overwhelm. I was genuinely struggling to keep all the balls in the air, and God's request felt like yet another demand on my depleted energy and time.

Still, I felt Him call, and He is ever patient and kind. *Have your lunch with Me quietly,* He said, *and then come sit and spend time. Give Me an hour. It will be worth your time.*

Begrudgingly, I "gave in." But I knew my attitude needed to change, and I noted in my heart one of my life's Scriptures: "Seek first his kingdom and his righteousness, and all these things will be given to you as well" (Matthew 6:33).

I apologized to God, went straight home, made some lunch, put on some worship and soaking music (I like to call time in stillness with God "soaking"), and sat down to spend the hour with Him. As I sat, I listened to Him. I prayed as prompted, and then I simply laid down in order to position myself to allow Him to speak to or just love me. To be honest, I felt nothing, I heard nothing, I saw nothing. As I lay still, I thought, *Well, this is a complete waste of time.* But in faith, I continued to rest.

After some time, in a "suddenly" moment, I saw a tiny brief flash of a picture in my mind's eye. I "saw" my daughter's pink retainer sitting on the pink and cream quilt on her bed.

I said to the Lord, *All right, I'll have a look, but You tell me when I need to get up to go. I will do this for You in faith even though I feel silly doing it. You know we couldn't find it up there before, don't You?*

Now, there's richness in just that statement: *You tell me when I'm to do this, and I will do it in faith.* Even though I was alone in my home, I felt silly doing it. Regardless, I soaked some more, and when I felt Him say "Go now," I went.

Walking into my daughter's bedroom, I looked at the bed. The retainer wasn't there. I pulled back the bedcovers and moved the pillows aside. It wasn't there. Disappointed and knowing I had to leave the house in ten minutes, I decided to recheck the pockets of her bathrobe. Nothing! I checked the pockets of her tracksuit pants. She'd worn them to swimming the night she said she'd lost it. Still nothing. I turned from the closet, feeling even more foolish as I thought, *It was just my imagination. I didn't really see anything from God.*

In that moment, self-condemnation flooded me, but I reminded myself that God was always good. I affirmed myself, knowing it would please Him that I'd tried. I'd responded in faith to what I thought I'd seen, and my stepping out in faith would delight Him, regardless.

As I was leaving my daughter's bedroom, I briefly glanced at a large basket that doubled as a bedside table. There, by her night-light, plain as day, was the retainer! Minutes before I had to leave to get a new one fitted, I'd found the missing retainer!

I gasped! Barely believing what I saw, I immediately thanked God and spent the next five minutes repenting for my lack of faith. I thanked Him profusely and repeatedly for His kindness and His faithfulness, and I then called my husband.

"Cancel the appointment," I said. I told Andrew the story, and he gasped too. He'd looked over the basket twice the night before. He swore to me it had not been there. I knew that had he looked, he would have seen it. It was so obvious when I saw it. It was obvious it was there!

God had said, *Give me an hour. It will be worth your time*, and now "seek first his kingdom and his righteousness, and all these things will be given to you as well" (Matthew 6:33) rang in my spirit. In spending an hour with God, I had redeemed an hour and a great deal of energy. There was no need to race to the orthodontist, and I saved a further hour for the follow-up appointment. In the one hour of time, God saved us an outlay of $450. But besides time redeemed and money saved, I'd gained time with my loving Father. Further, and this I particularly love, is how my children yet again saw their God come through for us as a family. He saw us in a time of need, and He came to our aid. It affirmed for us all that God is good!

YOU NEVER WASTE TIME WHEN YOU SPEND TIME WITH GOD

We should never consider time in stillness with God as wasted. Instead, it's the most important investment of time we can make. We all need to appreciate this on a much deeper level. It is certainly imperative that the body of Christ catch this truth. God isn't looking for minions to do His bidding. Rather, He's looking for sons and daughters to have a relationship with. He wants children who *know* His heart and understand *His* ways and, in doing so, reflect Him well.

The impact of spending time with God is immeasurable. It penetrates our very being with a quietness that leaks from the inside to the outside. I've spent time with Him and then gone about my day only for others to tell me there was something different about me. Strangers have stopped me to ask who and what I am. Others have advised they saw a light emanating from me, while others have felt a peace that transcends all understanding. These odd occurrences flow from time spent with Him, and they can happen to you, too, just by being you, permeated by Him.

JESUS IS OUR EXAMPLE

Of course, Jesus is the example we should all aspire to. Although constantly in communion with God, He regularly withdrew to spend time with the Father in solitude. He rose early when it was dark and went to a desolate place and prayed (Luke 4:42[1]). Prayer is a conversation with God. We speak while the other listens, then we listen while the other speaks. I'm sure Jesus listened at least as much as He spoke, if not more.

In times of personal challenge we see Him withdraw. On hearing the news of His cousin John the Baptist's death, Jesus withdraws in a boat to go to a solitary place (Matthew 14:13). No doubt He needs to be still and know that His Father is there with Him, for Him, loving Him in His grief. We read, though, that on seeing the needs of the people, He has compassion and temporarily suspends His own needs to minister to them (14:14). However, He doesn't fail to be still, for we read how after feeding the five thousand, He dismisses the crowds and goes up on a mountain (to a quiet place) to pray (14:23).

I suggest that if Jesus needed regular quiet time with His Father, then we do too. As Madame Guyon,[2] a seventeenth-century mystic, inferred so beautifully, the bees can only draw juice from the flowers by resting on them. Jesus withdrew to quiet places to pray, to be with His Father. He was still as He communed with His Father, and from that place He would emerge, knowing who He was as His Father's beloved Son. He was God's happy place. And from the place of solitude with His Father, Jesus would then go forth into the world He was called to in order to impact all those He encountered with the Father's love. Jesus went, representing His Father and sharing how all those He touched were also God's happy place.

This commission of representing the Father has now flowed to you and will deepen as you become aware of God's desire for you to know you are His happy place too. You are His beloved child. From you, the work of Jesus is multiplied, but first and foremost we need to respond to the command to be still and know that He is God.

The power of being still and knowing He is God is unfathomable. If we truly caught this, what could we do? Even as I write, I'm caught by the conviction of how good it is to "dwell in the house of the Lord forever" (Psalm 23:6). I have no doubt that as you lie down and seek the face of God, you will hear Him, know Him, and catch His heart for you. You will feel His attention and start to believe that you really are

His happy place. With this time spent, and with this knowledge—like Samuel and even like Jesus—you, with others by your side who also understand how much they're loved, will impact a nation with His goodness, for His glory.

By now you may ask, "But how?" In the chapters to come, we'll delve into these ideas. But for now, turn your face toward Jesus and allow Him to show you His Father, who wants to love you into the fullness of life.

QUESTIONS TO CONTEMPLATE

1. When have you been aware of being still with God, whether in a moment of worship, a time of reading the Scriptures, or even on a walk? Journal what that time was like, explaining what you saw, heard, felt, knew, tasted, or smelled.
2. Looking back, can you recognize moments when you were being called by God to spend time with Him but you didn't understand the call? Ask God what you can learn from those moments.
3. Thinking of the lessons learned from this chapter, what wisdom would you impart to others who are on this journey of learning to be still with God? Write down what worked for you, what challenges you faced in those moments, and how you would guide another in the process.

RESPONSE TO THE REVELATION

- **Action Step 1:** Set aside time this week to spend five to ten minutes with God and be still like Samuel. Have no agenda for this time. Just remove all distractions, lie down, and invite God to speak. After those times, journal what you saw, heard, felt, knew, tasted, or smelled. Become actively aware of the effect of your time being still with God. Ask Him to show how the atmosphere in your home has been

impacted. Take note of whether you're feeling more at peace within yourself. Do you have a deeper sense of hope or faith? Share your insights with your spouse or a trusted friend.
- **Action Step 2:** Like Habakkuk, bring a challenge you're facing before the Lord. Present it to Him, and then be still, waiting to see what God will say to you. He may not address your concern, but whatever He shows you or says to you, write it down and share your insights with your spouse or a trusted friend.

LET'S PRAY

Father, thank You for always being there for me, waiting for me to be still in Your presence. Help me carve out time to learn to be still, and help me discover You in the quietness of our time together. I ask to experientially know You, God, as Samuel came to know You. I ask for a deep revelation of Your goodness as I lie down to be still in Your presence and to help me see You as You are. I pray that as I learn to abide, I'll also recognize You more readily in encounters through my days. In the mighty name of Jesus I pray, amen.

5

THE NO-STRIVING ZONE

"God so loved the world that he gave his one and only Son, that whoever believes in him shall not perish but have eternal life."
John 3:16

UNCONDITIONAL LOVE REQUIRES nothing from the recipient. Given freely, expecting nothing in return, this type of love is the love God poured out upon all flesh through the gift of His Son, Jesus Christ. We need never strive nor perform for God's love; we are simply His loved ones—His happy place. We cannot earn God's love—indeed, our good works will never achieve it. Our exertions are useless to earn something already given so freely. God's love is a pure gift. And remember, Christ gave His life before the beginning of time. Therefore, it is timeless, a gift given to us before our very existence.

God's love, reflected in the gift of Jesus, stretches through time, beyond time, and before time. Therefore, when we read how God so loved us that He gave His only Son, we can know He freely gave us Jesus before any of our own good works could even exist. God also gives only with our very best interests in mind. We need never strive to receive it or to keep it, for the gift of Jesus has no strings attached.

There's no expectation of performance, or payment "in kind." A gift is only a gift when there's no presumption of anything in return.

I caught an understanding of this concept many years ago when my daughter was very ill. Now, my love for my children has never been transactional. It's not about how good they make me feel or look or how well they serve me. And it must never be about my dreams, goals, plans, or vision for my life or be my dreams, goals, plans, or vision for their life. Rather, I see my parental role as one of facilitating my children's God-given dreams from the place of their freedom to choose. I support their pursuit of godly purpose with no strings attached. Unlike God, I'm not a perfect parent, but I do my best, giving my children choices while guiding them as best I can.

But let me share the story of how I suddenly realized I existed in a no-striving zone.

GOD IS GOOD STORY: SIMPLY BECAUSE HE LOVES US

My daughter, Rebekah, is a joy-filled, vibrant, kind, quirky girl. She always has been. She has a leadership gift, with healing, prophecy, and worship thrown into the mix. When she was six years old and brand-new at elementary school, she developed a stomach virus. She vomited continuously for ten days straight. Sick day and night, she lost well over 10 percent of her weight. We were all exhausted and deeply concerned for her. Not knowing what was causing the illness, I fasted, prayed, and sought God's advice.

God, what is it? Where is the breakthrough? What is going on?

On the tenth day she finally stopped vomiting, and the illness resolved as quickly as it began. But during those ten days, she lay listlessly on the couch, barely able to lift her head. I felt quite desperate. We didn't know what to do. The doctors said the next step was the hospital. We knew this could not continue and soon would need ongoing medical help.

I looked at Rebekah despairingly, and as I did, God spoke. *You see her? Do you see her! Why do you want her well? Why do you want her to be healthy?* His tone was urgent, insistent.

Because I love her, I said, perplexed.

To me, it seemed obvious why I would want her well, and I felt puzzled and even a little irritated that He should ask. Then His response came rushing at me, forcing my thought processes further.

Do you want her well so she can push a vacuum cleaner around to clean the house for you? Do you want her to unload the dishwasher and do some jobs for you? Would you like her well so she can hang out the washing? Do you want her to perform well to make you look good?

Shocked at this line of questioning, I quickly realized the direction He was going. *No, I just want her well. I want her well so she can be who she is—a joy-filled, sassy, vibrant, funny, quirky little girl who loves to sing and dance.*

Still insistent, He responded, *OK, so that's what I want for My children too.*

Ponder this for a moment. God doesn't want you well, healed, and saved so you can serve Him. He wants you well and fulfilling your purpose so you can thrive in life! Makes sense, doesn't it? After all, Jesus came to give us life and to give it to us abundantly (John 10:10). But what does an abundant life look like to you? To me, it looks like discovering why I'm me, what my kingdom purpose is, and then fulfilling it. The abundant life Jesus came to give is one that brings great joy, and with it a deep sense of fulfillment. It's finding our gifting, our measure, our sphere, our passions, and then living from those as we affect the world around us for good.

FULLY ME, FULLY YOU

If we can catch the concept in Matthew 7:11, we'll understand the depths of His love: "If you, then, though you are evil, know how to give good gifts to your children, how much more will your Father in heaven give good gifts to those who ask him!" If we only want the best for our children, then how much more will our Father in heaven want the same for us? He is a good God! He is a kind God! He's a better parent than you or I will ever be! If it's not good, it's simply not God!

A loving parent doesn't think *What can my child do for me?* but

What can I do for my child? How can I assist my child to step into their unique life design? In doing so, our children will live a life filled with joy. Now note, I didn't say have a happy life. Happiness is a transient feeling, whereas a life of joy is a life where we live from a much deeper place of fulfillment. It's contentment amid trials and blessings alike. In this place, joy is discovered within trials *and* blessings.

Yes, joy is present despite trials. Therefore, we need not ask what we can do for God. It's simply a matter of, without striving, being still and knowing Him. It's about catching the wind of who God is, and in that exchange, catch the fragrance of who we are too. It's *Who am I in God?* It's from that place that we can step into a joy-filled life, full of kingdom purpose, flowing from kingdom identity. We rest knowing we are His happy place and from there we go.

Like any terrific father, God draws out our truest selves. It's in our time with Him, in the secret place, that we discover Him and in Him we discover ourselves. In this place, we abide in Him, He abides in us, and we abide with Him as we do life together. It's therefore from "fullness" that we flow. From that place, we can't help but spill out into the world. In that place, with Him, we become completely ourselves but completely in Him and full of Him too. In that place, we drink the living waters, and streams of living waters flow through us to others.

I must also highlight a further important fact. It's not about *Less of me, more of You, Lord*. Conceptually, this sounds very spiritual, but it's flawed thinking. Rather, it's *Fully me, fully You*. Fully me in God's glory, completely me as the person He's made me to be and full (overflowing) with Him. As we catch this, we spill out into society simply as we go about our day. We don't have to strive to perform for Him to see us, to love us, to make Him pleased. We never need to strive to be His children; we *are* His children. It's not *good girl, good boy, therefore you're in; bad girl, bad boy, therefore you're out*. We are His children, and He loves us! Remember Mark 1:11: "You are My beloved Son, in whom I am well pleased" (NKJV). He's already pleased with His children. We are His happy place.

His love for us also has nothing to do with how much time we spend with Him—although, as I discussed last chapter, hanging out with the creator of the universe is never a waste of time. Of course, the more time we spend, the more we behold Him and the more like Him we become. So being more like Him through spending time with Him is a great idea, but we don't spend that time to be accepted, loved, or approved. We already have His acceptance, love, and approval.

It's also not what we do *for* Him that brings blessing to us. Rather, we're blessed because of who He is. He loves us because of who He is. It has nothing to do with us, but it also has everything to do with us, for we are the apple of His eye!

God gave me a beautiful example as I taught this concept years ago. It came in a moment when a memory flooded my heart and soul.

GOD IS GOOD STORY: HE DESIRES TO BE WITH YOU

When I was young, I played three musical instruments. While I was the most proficient on the violin, I had a particular affinity for the harp. To fulfill my little girl's dream, my parents stretched their finances when I was about ten years old and bought me a full-sized concert harp. It was beautiful. With the most magnificent sound, I needed little skill to generate the most beautiful music.

I distinctly remember a moment with my father, well before I'd made an articulated decision for Christ. I was about fifteen or sixteen years old, and as I practiced on my harp, I was suddenly aware of my earthly father's presence in the room. He had silently entered and appeared to be looking at the many books in our extensive bookshelves. It was a common thing for him to do, but I knew he wasn't really looking. It was a little odd.

I stopped playing and said, "Dad, did you want to talk to me about something?"

"No," he said.

So I kept playing, and he continued "looking" at the books. Sensing the moment, I stopped playing again.

"Dad, are you sure? Did you want to tell me something?"

Looking a little sheepish and even a little teary, he said, "No,

Bethie. I just love being with you. I wanted to be in the same room as you and listen to you play."

Although not perfect, my father seemed able to communicate how much he loved me. I was fortunate that way. With a look, a smile, a rub on my cheek with the back of his hand, I knew I was loved. With a story of how glad he was that I was alive, and that I was his daughter, his eyes would mist up with affection and love. I knew that I knew my dad loved me. He was a gentle soul, and his love ran deep.

At this moment, he wanted to be quiet and present in the same room with me, even though he said nothing at all. And I just needed to be me in the moment. There was no striving to be accepted by my father—he was simply present, loving me, as I did my thing.

Years later, well after my father had passed, God reminded me of this moment. I was teaching a group about practicing God's presence (or, again, as I like to call it, soaking) when this memory flooded back with a profound revelation. I knew that I knew my earthly father had loved me completely in that moment. And I knew that I knew he wanted to be with me for nothing more than to just be with me. He showed me he wanted to be with me because he loved me. There was no reason other than love.

God the Father then pierced my heart with a deep understanding that He is the same, only better. Sometimes He just wants to be with us and simply desires us to be with Him. Nothing more, nothing less. Just being together makes God glad. After all, we are His happy place!

Sometimes we're "still" with God and He speaks. No striving involved. We listen, and He talks. Think of our discussion about Samuel, who laid down in the temple to listen. Think also of Jesus retreating to spend time with His Father. The revelatory rivers will flow in those moments as we are with God. Other times, God will be with us and say nothing. These quiet moments are moments of gentle, quiet bliss. Whether or not we feel Him, He's there. The impact of these quiet moments are equally profound, for the outflow from the overflow of these times is deeply impactful for us.

These times will also affect those we meet as we go about our day, even if we're no longer aware of God's presence. We don't need to strive to be convincing as a Christian in these times. We're simply ourselves, and from there we flow. We never need to strive to be with God, for we live in the no-striving zone.

GOD IS LOVE, AND HE SO LOVES

God's love expresses His very nature, for Love is who He is. He gives with an unselfish, pure love, free of conditions and expectations. We, in turn, simply accept the gift, and in that acceptance, the gift flows to us. I'm sure God hopes we'll respond to His gift well. Naturally, when we give a gift, we hope the recipient will receive it with gladness of heart. We hope they'll unwrap it with joyful anticipation and a full appreciation of what it is, especially if it costs us something. But that's the thing about gifts—the recipient is free to accept it or not. They don't strive to receive; they simply receive. They might not like the gift; they might scorn it, waste it, or let it lay to ruin through ignorance or misuse. But what makes a gift a gift is that it's given freely, with no strings attached.

So the unwrapping of the gift of Jesus should never be accompanied by a performance mindset. Rather, He is to be received and assimilated into us and our lives. As we appreciate the gift of Jesus, we will unwrap His significance for ourselves and for those around us. Once we catch who He really is, that He came to truly set us free, it's only natural to flow into the fullest version of ourselves, and with that, our kingdom purpose will grow.

In my exchange with God while my daughter was ill, I saw how as her mother, I wanted her well. Indeed, I wanted her to thrive, and I was looking forward to watching her shine as Rebekah, my daughter whom I love and adore. Similarly, God is our Father, and He wants to be with us and watch us thrive and grow into all He's created us to be. As we learn to be all He's created us to be, we'll be capable of doing all He's created us to do. And doing so will bring us the most satisfaction and joy. If we will just be with Him, the rest will flow.

In both exchanges with God, in my understanding through Rebekah's illness and my time with my father as I played the harp, I also caught the truth that I could just be me. God adored me, and He loved me just because! I could sit for the rest of my life and do nothing for Him, and He wouldn't love me any less. And He wouldn't love me more. Love is who He is, therefore, He loves, and I would continue to be His happy place.

NO STRIVING NEEDED TO RECEIVE GOD'S GIFT

Let's turn our thoughts to the crucifixion scene in Luke 23:39–43, where we find two thieves being crucified with Jesus:

> One of the criminals who hung there hurled insults at him: "Aren't you the Messiah? Save yourself and us!" But the other criminal rebuked him. "Don't you fear God," he said, "since you are under the same sentence? We are punished justly, for we are getting what our deeds deserve. But this man has done nothing wrong." Then he said, "Jesus, remember me when you come into your kingdom." Jesus answered him, "Truly I tell you, today you will be with me in paradise."

The second thief merely asks to be remembered and Jesus responds, "You're in!" There is no fanfare, no baptism (in water, fire, or tongues), and no ministry feats. There were no works at all, and yet Jesus receives him.

We ask, say "Thank you," and the rest will fall into place.

As we assimilate the gift of Jesus, we take Him on, we take Him in, we absorb Him, and He absorbs us. Like a sponge, we soak Him in. As we step into Him, we understand that not only is He the access point to God but that He also finishes our faith. He is all at once our entry point and our destination. In Jesus, we live and flourish. Jesus gives, and we receive. There is no performance, no striving, nor expectation for anything in return, and yet love desires the best for a person. God's desire is greater union with us, and union with Him will always bring a fullness of life. With union will come a call to mature, and with maturity, our roles will change. But for now, understand, we abide and simply flow. We live in the no-striving zone.

TO ABIDE AND FLOW

In John 15:4, Jesus said, "Remain in me, as I also remain in you. No branch can bear fruit by itself; it must remain in the vine. Neither can you bear fruit unless you remain in me."

Remaining in Jesus is an act of being without trying. It's not something we "do," although "doing" will flow from that place of being. Rather, we are "being" in Him, because once we've said yes, we *are* in Him. Then from that being in Him, we do. Can you see there is no striving because we're simply being, and from being we do, because it's who we are, not what we do?

Let's use a natural example. Think of an orange tree. The orange tree is an orange tree. It doesn't try or strive to be an orange tree. It's just an orange tree, and orange trees do what an orange tree does by abiding in the soil, drawing nutrients, allowing water to soak its roots, and being. Fruit comes from that place of being, or abiding. There's no squeezing out fruit. The orange tree doesn't force fruit. Rather, fruit comes because it is what it is—an orange tree. The fruit comes through abiding and simply being what it already is.

We're the same. It's just that somehow we got ourselves all muddled up. As we learn to "be" before we "do," we create fruit just by being who we are in God. He wants us healthy first and foremost, but we don't even need to wait to heal. We simply abide and be, and as we do, fruit comes.

Please note that nothing about this is transactional. It's a gift, free flowing from heaven to earth. Jesus keeps giving an inexhaustible outflow of living waters. He's the ultimate no-striving zone, where we receive the flow from Him and then we flow with Him, in Him, to others. We receive and we give away. There's always more. Our source never runs dry.

So often we ask God, *What can I do for You?* The very question suggests striving and performance. There's such an emphasis on doing things for God—performance over relationship. However, what God desires is us. He wants us to abide in Him and rest in Him to allow us to be saturated so we can flow with His goodness—not through trying, but just through being who we already are.

MARY HAS CHOSEN THE BETTER THING—TO BE BEFORE WE DO

In essence, we all need to learn to "be" and then practice "being" who we already are. We're not human *doings*; our identity is not in what we do. We're human *beings*. We learn to be ourselves by being at the feet of Jesus. It's here, in this place, that we learn to go in and out. Knowing we're always in Him, we choose to spend time with Him just because. We don't live to perform for Jesus, but to be in a relationship with Him. As we spend time with Him, He unravels the world's concepts of what we must do to be a Christian.

As children adopted into the family of God, we learn what delights Him—us! Still surprised? Don't be, for we really are His happy place! From that place of acceptance, He can then speak to us about who He's created us to be and what treasure He's deposited within us that He's calling out. As we are fully ourselves, we shine, and in doing so, we bring Him glory!

A beautiful example of how striving doesn't impress God is in Luke 10:38–42:

> As Jesus and his disciples were on their way, he came to a village where a woman named Martha opened her home to him. She had a sister called Mary, who sat at the Lord's feet listening to what he said. But Martha was distracted by all the preparations that had to be made. She came to him and asked, "Lord, don't you care that my sister has left me to do the work by myself? Tell her to help me!"
>
> "Martha, Martha," the Lord answered, "you are worried and upset about many things, but few things are needed—or indeed only one. Mary has chosen what is better, and it will not be taken away from her."

We can see that in this moment, the best thing Mary could do was simply sit at the feet of Jesus. She needed to be with Him, perhaps listen to Him, rather than be busy about the many tasks that no doubt needed attention. From this place of being, we will affect the world with ease. We need not be a Martha, striving to complete the many ministry tasks or even the worldly tasks on our to-do lists. If we choose to put striving away and sit at the feet of Jesus, from there all life will flow.

THE IMPACT WILL FLOW FORTH

Sometimes when I've arrived at school pickup after spending time with God, after sitting at the feet of Jesus, people have said, "Oh my gosh, you feel so peaceful." They don't know I have many thoughts raging in my head, because I'm one who's thinking, thinking, thinking, and peace is the furthest thing from my mind. One woman even said, "I always feel so peaceful when I'm around you." The irony was that in this moment I was far from a peaceful place in my head.

I soon realized a pattern was emerging. After abiding with and in God, others could feel Him flowing from me. This woman felt peace because I'd been with the person Peace. I'd been hanging out with the One who loved me, with the One who saw me, with the One who knew me, and His fragrance emitted Peace.

Another person approached me at school pickup time and said, "There's a light coming out of you. What are you?"

"Really?" I said. "I'm a Christian, and I believe you're seeing God in me."

We had quite a chat about what being a Christian meant. At the end of our discussion, she said, "I've seen nothing quite like it. It's amazing."

In this season, I was collecting my children from school activities many times a week, and so many of my interactions centered in those times. One afternoon, a woman at my children's ballet class said, "I don't know what it is about you, but I desperately want to stand next to you. Every time we're at pickup together, I want to be near you.

The problem is," she continued, "I want to cry whenever I get too near."

She knew I was a Christian. I'd prayed for her many times. On one such occasion, I prayed when she was injured at a concert, and she was healed and repeated her observation: "It's just so bizarre. I always want to cry when I'm near you."

"Well, that's Jesus," I replied. "It's not me that you can feel, but Jesus. I'm sure I wouldn't impress you if you stood next to just me. But in me you can feel the One who's saturated me in His presence. He changes the atmosphere. That's what you can feel when you want to cry."

In all these interactions no striving was involved. I didn't squeeze out good fruits, I was just me, overflowing with Jesus.

You, too, don't need to do anything to carry Jesus into society. Just be with Him, and you'll leak as you go! You don't need to be healed, ramped up on worship, or prayed up in tongues to be saturated with Him. There's no requirement to perform. You don't need to be perfect. You just need to say yes to Him and thoroughly be yourself. (Remember, you're in a constant state of "1:11." You're His beloved daughter or beloved son, in whom He's well pleased.) God then reaches out through you to those to whom He wants to make Himself known. It's a natural thing for Him to do, because He loves them, too, and after all, He's the living waters springing up that flow from your inner being. He wants everyone to know they're His happy place.

The kingdom of heaven really is a no-striving zone. Jesus is a gift, and His love is absolutely unconditional. You receive Him, thank Him, and turn to gaze at Him. And as you see Him, from the place of acceptance, you can rest and flow. It's quite simple: "God so loved the world that he gave his one and only Son, that whoever believes in him shall not perish but have everlasting life" (John 3:16).

You don't need to perform for God's love or salvation. Salvation is a gift freely given to you. As you say, "Thank you," simply trust that the rest will fall into place.

QUESTIONS TO CONTEMPLATE

1. What awareness of a peace that "transcends all understanding" (Philippians 4:7) have you experienced? What has been the result when you've stopped striving and stilled your inner busyness?
2. Ask God to show you where you might have been striving for His approval or for the approval of others. What does He have to say to you about that? Journal what He says.
3. When have people ever noted something different about you? What did they say? If you have never had that happen, journal how you might respond to them in a gentle, inviting way.

RESPONSE TO THE REVELATION

- **Action Step 1:** This week allocate some time each day to sit at the feet of Jesus. Ask Him what is on His heart and listen quietly. Allow the stillness and gentleness of His presence minister to you and slow you down enough to catch the truth that He wants time *with* you over all your good works and striving.
- **Action Step 2:** While sitting at the feet of Jesus, ask Him to show you where and when to arise with Him and go. Be willing to arise from where you think He is, or even should be, and go out to meet Him throughout your day. He'll be there going about His Father's business. Be aware if He's wanting to reach those around you, and ask Him what He'd like you to do as you walk by His side.

LET'S PRAY

Father, I've strived for Your love and affection. I accept Your gift of love as a child and simply say, "Thank you." I thank You that You've laid out a plan and a purpose for me that is a joy to step into. I thank You that You require no striving on my part to fulfill all the purposes You've set before me to complete. I lay down all my busyness at Your feet to simply be with You and choose to enjoy the journey ahead.

Thank You that Your yes to all You have for me is assured, and I say "Amen" to Your plans laid before me. I choose peaceful stillness within my inner being and call forth, "Fully my kingdom me, Lord, filled to overflowing with You." In Jesus' mighty name I pray, amen.

6

ABIDING IN MY GOD SPACE

*And it shall come to pass afterward,
that I will pour out my spirit upon all flesh.*
Joel 2:28 KJV

LIFE in the twenty-first century is loud, driven, and incessant. Phone calls, messages, emails, texts, and reminders constantly speak of busy lives as we succumb to the lie that busyness equates success, satisfaction, importance—even status. We ignore the cry of our hearts where deep calls to deep, and we reach for the sugar rush our busy lives bring us, missing that there's something of greater significance at hand. We all know intuitively that luxury and garb will never satisfy our deepest yearning, and yet we still chase them.

Christians can be just as caught up with the rush—meetings, numbers, programs, performance, boxes to tick, and people to please. We can also miss the mark of what our Christian faith is all about, or rather, *whom* our Christian walk is about. Faith in God, through His Son, Jesus Christ, was never meant to be a job description but an adventure with the most loving, kind, fun, generous, and hope-filled individual you can imagine.

And an adventure it is! However, if you're on an adventure, it's always wise to keep sight of where your guide and companion is as you go forth into the unknown. You need to know where he is for you at any given moment and that you can rely on him given a pinch of trouble. And I'm delighted to say you can when your guide and fellow adventurer is God, for we all have a place where He is for us at any given moment. We have a space where we can know He'll be on any day, in any place, at any time.

The delightful thing is that *all* human beings have this place, which, once found, will give us faith for the journey ahead. Yes, *all* human beings have what is called a "God space," a place where we can encounter God for ourselves. Science supports it, the Scriptures declare it, and the evidence of many are witness to it. And once we learn how to find it and access it for ourselves, we can all learn to abide in our God space, and in that place all else fades away.

WE ALL HAVE A GOD SPACE—THE SCIENCE SAYS IT ALL

Years ago I was fortunate to hear Dr. Diane Divett speak at our church.[1] With a master's degree in education and sweeping expertise in child and adolescent mental health, she was completing her PhD when she spoke. I thoroughly enjoyed what she had to say and found her approach grounded and well researched.

Dr. Divett shared how all human beings, even atheists, have what she described as a "God space." She discovered this by chance, and upon researching the phenomenon, she completed a subsequent PhD on the topic. She explained that a God space is where people can identify that God is present for them. She said it's where our awareness of God can increase as we experience Him for ourselves. As I listened and subsequently learned more, I came to understand that we can practice finding and going to our God space for ourselves, and I now believe that as we do, we can not only become more aware of Him in our quiet times but as we go about our daily life.

She also told the story of how she first discovered this phenomenon. She was counseling a man with cystic fibrosis when she asked him, "Where is God for you right now?" He sat near a window and explained it felt like God was the light coming down upon him. He then breathed deeply. Dr. Divett asked him what was happening, and he said, "It's like I'm on a pump and I can breathe."

For someone with symptomatic cystic fibrosis, this statement was extraordinary. Cystic fibrosis affects the lungs in such a way that sufferers often struggle for breath. But in that moment, Dr. Divett's patient could take long, deep breaths.

On a subsequent visit, the same patient described God as being there for him like liquid honey pouring down his throat. Dr. Divett encouraged him to keep going to these God spaces—to the pump and the honey—and each time he did, he was aware of God. He described a change and an ability to breathe with greater ease each time he was aware of where God was for him. The difference in his breathing was so pronounced that Dr. Divett suggested he should keep doing what he was doing every day. He did, and at the time of her telling his story, he was the longest surviving cystic fibrosis patient she was aware of in New Zealand. In effect, what this man learned was how to "practice the presence" of God. He had learned to go to his God space, and of course, in that place, healing flowed.

Upon this discovery, Dr. Divett explored this concept in her doctoral thesis.[2]

What Dr. Divett discovered and now teaches is that we all have a place we can access called our God space. It's simply about becoming aware of where God is for us as we sit still and know that He is God. It's in this place that we discover how much God loves us—how we are His personal happy place.

THIS IS THAT—JOEL PROPHESIED GOD'S SPIRIT WOULD BE AVAILABLE TO US ALL

The research conducted by Dr. Divett is wonderful and provides grounded scientific proof of what Scripture has already told us. In Acts 2:1–4, we read about the outpouring of the Holy Spirit at the time of Pentecost. Witnesses hear a sudden, violent wind and see what seems to be flames of fire resting upon people. The Holy Spirit fills the disciples, and many speak in strange tongues. Chaos prevails. The spectacle causes some to be amazed, and others perplexed. Still others mock and claim drunkenness is the cause. In this setting, Peter stands to clearly articulate what's happening. He says, "These people are not drunk, as you suppose. It's only nine in the morning! No, this is what was spoken by the prophet Joel" (Acts 2:15–16). He then proceeds to quote Joel 2:28–29:

> In the last days, God says, I will pour out my Spirit on all people. Your sons and daughters will prophesy, your young men will see visions, your old men will dream dreams. Even on my servants, both men and women, I will pour out my Spirit in those days, and they will prophesy. I will show wonders in the heavens above and signs on the earth below, blood and fire and billows of smoke. The sun will be turned to darkness and the moon to blood before the coming of the great and glorious day of the Lord. And everyone who calls on the name of the Lord will be saved. (Acts 2:17–21)

Joel saw a day when God would pour His Spirit out on *all flesh*, and he prophesied that when this happened, God's sons and daughters would prophesy, young men would see visions, and old men would dream dreams. Peter identified Pentecost as that day fulfilled. God's Spirit was poured out on all people and continues to be to this day.

Written in a form of Hebraic poetry, Joel mentions men, but he includes outliers too—women, young, old, slave, free. The language is intentional and adopts a poetic structure called parallelism that, by inference, incorporates the extremes mentioned and everything in between. In other words, this is for everyone! It means this outpouring of prophecy, dreams, and visions is for all those mentioned and anyone in between. These beautiful gifts are for all believers.

But let's back up for a moment and look at the line "I will pour out my Spirit on all people." This line is significant. If we follow it to its logical conclusion, "all people" means "all people," therefore God's Spirit has been poured out on all humankind. Let me draw it out a little more. In those days (from the days of Pentecost) God has poured out His Spirit on "all people." Other translations say, "on all flesh" (Joel 2:28 NKJV and KJV). This was a radical concept for the Jews hearing these words. To even contemplate the idea that a gentile (a non-Jewish person) could receive such an outpouring from God was blasphemous. But this statement of Joel's is even more radical than including gentile believers, because it's stating if you have flesh, if you are human, you qualify!

God has poured out His Spirit on all humankind so that they might know Him. He desires a relationship with *every* human being, and so He has poured out His Spirit to all humankind. *All* can encounter Him—believer and pre-believer alike. Indeed, an encounter is essential to salvation, for how else would people come to Jesus Christ if not by the Holy Spirit? But not all know how to recognize Him when He comes. So by extension, believers *and* pre-believers alike can encounter the Spirit of God.

Let's make something clear, though. An encounter doesn't equate salvation. But it does mean God's Spirit is available to all. He's reaching out, engaging with people, inviting them into His embrace. I believe this is what occurred when I encountered Love as a teenager while I played my violin. It was a presence, a person, who entered my room. A person whose presence I now recognize as the Holy Spirit. I experienced a love so profound that I wept as I played. I didn't recognize Him at *that* moment, but had someone helped point the way, I would have said yes!

So let's sum it up. From the day of Pentecost, God's Spirit has been poured out on all flesh, and His Spirit continues to pour out today. Each of us can learn to recognize Him and respond to Him. Joel prophesied this reality in Joel 2:28, and Peter recognized that Joel's prophecy was fulfilled at Pentecost. Believers and even pre-believers can know and experience the truth that God's Spirit pours forth on all flesh. Note, I'm not talking about prophesying, rather that the Spirit of God is being poured out across the globe. So Scripture shows us that all human beings can encounter God, and now, with Dr. Divett's PhD research, modern science backs up this contention too.

But let's not leave it there. Let's discuss the basics of how you can find your God space.

FINDING YOUR GOD SPACE

We can all find our own God space; Scripture and science both witness this fact. We can do it by gently quieting our minds as we take a few deep breaths and ask, *God, where are You for me right now?* Then as we gently rest, we will become aware of God by asking ourselves, *What am I seeing, hearing, sensing, or knowing at this moment?"*

You may sense Him above you, below you, beside you, all around you, or even within you. He may be in a geographical space, across the room, toward the horizon, or even sitting in a chair across from you. You might notice a sensation of warmth or extreme peace. You might feel love, hope, joy, or faith. We follow these thoughts, these knowings, even pictures and sensations, and make inquiries of ourselves.

Dr. Divett then encourages us to explore the space. We note what the space is like, where it is, how it makes us feel. Wherever God is for you in the moment, He is. Don't over analyze it; just allow it to be. Whatever you experience, though, will always reflect *who* He is, and He is love. If you see or feel anything but His kindness, I encourage you to look again, ask again, and explore what you see, hear, feel, taste, smell, know. But rather than try to teach the theory, let me show you through a story of my own.

GOD IS GOOD STORY: IN FINDING HER GOD SPACE, A PRODIGAL DAUGHTER COMES HOME

Heading to the local shopping center, I leaned into the heart of God. Then feeling led to walk through Myer (a local department store much like Walmart), I made my way there.

I stopped to buy a T-shirt for my husband and a beautiful woman waited on me. Feeling God's heart for her, I asked if I could pray a blessing. She agreed. I prayed a tenfold return on the blessing she'd been, and although I felt nothing as I prayed, I trusted God would follow through on my words. I then felt God prompt me to go upstairs through the department store, so I headed toward the escalators.

Now, I'm going to stop here. It's important that you start to "catch" the language. I *felt* prompted to go upstairs through the department store. Through this time, God is leading my steps. I've learned to find where God is for me throughout my day. While Dr. Divett's idea of God spaces is to be used at times when we sit and intentionally ask Him where He is for us in a given moment, I also engage with Him as I go about my day, mixing my prophetic gifting with my gift of discernment and healing. I call it "being a Christian." It's normal Christian living.

Actually, it's more simple than even that. It's simply "being me," for we were all born for this way of life. We can all live life constantly chatting to God. When I'm out and about, I can be aware of Him in multiple ways. Sometimes I feel Him in my heart, leading me through a deep feeling of compassion for someone. Other times He speaks to me through external prompts. In this instance, I *heard* a small inner voice and *felt* a "hunch" of where I should go next. The small inner voice sounds like my own thoughts, but I've learned to distinguish the gentle whisperings of God's ideas from my own. Then I simply listen as I go and respond to His leading.

So let's continue.

As I went up the escalator, I "coincidently" saw a woman I'd prayed for some time before. She had Grave's disease, a thyroid condition causing her right eye to bulge. She'd told me she could eventually go blind.

I called out to her, "How are you?"

"I'm losing more of my sight," she responded as she pointed to her eye.

"Would you like a quick prayer?"

"Yes, absolutely."

I spun around at the top of the escalator and headed back down to pray.

"Can I place my hand on the right side of your face?" I asked her, then did so once she agreed.

As I prayed for her to be healed, I thanked God for the promises we all have as believers in Jesus Christ and referenced Mark 16:17–18 and Matthew 11:5. "I thank you, Lord, that as I lay hands upon this beautiful woman, she will be healed, and that these signs shall follow me as a believer—'the blind receive sight.'"

She told me she felt something in her eye as I prayed, and I laughed. "Your eye looks less bulgy than it was before. Go check it out in the bathroom."

"I'm going to," she replied, then excitedly raced off to see.

I completed a few more chores, receiving God's blessing and favor everywhere I went. It was simply a lovely time, aware of God being with me in what Dr. Divett would call my God space.

Nearing the end of my time, I then felt the need to head straight back through the third floor of the department store to go home. *I'm going to stop for a takeout coffee. I'll enjoy that*, I thought.

As I headed through the third floor, God reminded me my son needed new pajamas. I smiled as He did so. I was feeling great. This limited shopping time was turning out to be an excellent time of prayer, and I was quickly ticking off chores. Blessing and favor were all rolled up in one! It was a "smorgasbord outing" with God.

I found the pajamas, and next in line to be served, I stood with my purchase at the cash register. An older lady beside me was having trouble with her credit card, and I noticed her rising anxiety. I was definitely looking forward to my cuppa before heading home, and I hoped her problem would be sorted out quickly.

But I was also listening to the heart of God, and before I could think, I blurted, "Let me pay for that" as I handed over my credit card. The woman—I'll call her Vivian—gratefully accepted, and as the transaction went through, she started telling me about her grandkids and cried.

"Wait for me to finish making my purchase and I'll pray for you," I said.

I briefly explained I was a Christian as she waited by my side, and with the purchase complete, I turned to pray. Vivian wept quietly under the anointing. As soon as I stopped, she poured more of her heart out. I leaned into God's heart again, into my God space, and I knew I needed to write off the rest of my morning. *God, You'll need to redeem the time*, I said to Him silently, knowing this woman was far more important than my own plans.

"Let's have a coffee," I said, still wanting that cuppa.

As we stood in line where coffee was sold in the store, she told me more of her story. Then with drinks in hand, we found a couch and sat down. Vivian also shared she had arthritis, so I held her hand and commanded the arthritis to go. As I did, I felt God ask me to help her find where God was for her. I was to help her find her God space, with onlookers passing by.

I stepped her through the initial process and then asked, "Where is God for you right now?"

"God is way up in heaven, and I'm way down here with you!" she said.

"Hey, would you like to ask Him to come closer?" I asked.

"Yes."

"Well, ask Him to come closer."

So she did!

"OK, where is He now?" I asked.

"Oh, He's on the couch opposite us."

"Do you want Him to come closer?" I asked again.

"Yes."

"Well, ask Him to come closer."

As she did, she cried some more, and the anointing grew thick, heavy, and strong.

I asked her again, "Where is God for you right now?"

"Jesus is kneeling right in front of me. He's forgiven me," she said, still crying.

I gently suggested she tell Him all she wanted to tell Him. To let Him know all that was in her heart.

Vivian wept a little more before she spoke. "Jesus, I'm so sorry for being away from You."

I then felt prompted by God to say, "Would you like to ask Him into your heart?"

"I did that a long time ago," she replied.

Checking in with God, I felt Him suggest I ask a different question. "Well, would you like to ask Him in again, afresh?"

"Yes!"

So there in the middle of our local department store, Vivian recommitted her life to Jesus, asking Him to wash her clean and fill her heart anew. We talked a little more about the Holy Spirit, and I prayed, telling any demonic presence to leave and never return. I then asked the Holy Spirit to fill her completely.

In finding her God space, a prodigal daughter encountered Jesus and came home. She shook a little, weeping as He healed her broken heart. The anointing remained thick and strong. Indeed, each time she invited Jesus to come closer, the anointing had grown more powerful. It was so strong that I also shook as I felt the Holy Spirit swirl.

"I can feel a tingling in and on my hands," she said.

Again, on the prompting of the Holy Spirit, I prayed for an impartation of the gift of healing. I offered first, to be sure Vivian wanted it, and she immediately agreed, explaining her husband was in a wheelchair due to a medical condition. She wanted to go home to pray for his healing.

We talked about church, and I gave her my number. I mentioned I was going to a seminar where the last time I'd heard the itinerant minister speak, I'd seen an arm grow out.

"My husband's arm is shorter than the other!" she exclaimed.

"No way!" I said. "My mentioning that to you is *not* a coincidence."

I told her that her husband could receive healing for his arm, and she said she wanted to get back to church. I made a few suggestions as we talked a while longer.

It was eventually time to head home, and as we walked through the store together, I told her she was an answer to my prayer that the prodigals and orphans would come home. I affirmed God loved her so much that He'd sent someone to call her back to Him. As I went to leave, I gave her a hug and a kiss.

"It was so strange," Vivian said. "During the entire time, people watched us." She explained a man walked past us who looked exactly like a Christian man who'd cared for her when she had postpartum depression. I pointed out again that God was on her case. It was no coincidence. God had set her up, but He'd also set me up to be there in the moment of need. Vivian encountered God and found her God space. He was always nearby; she simply needed to look to see. He was there waiting, happy to come close, as close as she would allow. And as she invited Him, He responded with love. At that moment, she knew His love. He healed Vivian's broken heart and invited her back home. She had always been His happy place!

Understanding the concept of God spaces is powerful. We all have one, and when found, healing often comes—hearts mend and love flows. As we engage where God is for us, we start to learn that *we* indeed are His happy place. To encounter the God of love and be equipped to see Him for ourselves is liberating, but to *really* catch the truth of how delighted He is with us is profound. Once caught, we can share the concept with others and liberate them to see that they are also God's delight and desire. They, too, are God's happy place! He really is the God who sees us and loves us enough to call us home. It helps us all to know how to find our God space—believer, prodigal, prebeliever, and even our leaders.

My husband and I shared this concept with a church leader, and the impact in his life and in the lives of the congregation he led was beautiful and profound. Let me share the story with you.

WE ALL NEED TO KNOW HIS LOVE

In 2020, during the hard lockdowns in Melbourne, Australia, due to COVID-19, Andrew and I reached out to a pastor living in another Australian state. I'll call him Stephen. Unbeknownst to us, Stephen was having a tough time. Our original intent was to find someone to support us as we supported others, and so we suggested a Zoom call. But during the call it quickly became apparent he was the one in need.

As we chatted, I felt I should talk to him about God spaces. I wanted to help him tangibly reconnect with God. Stephen intellectually knew God loved him, but he simply wasn't feeling it. I briefly explained the science behind God spaces, and after I walked him through the initial steps, I asked where God was for him. He said Jesus was standing on the other side of the room. At the suggestion of the Holy Spirit, I adopted a similar approach to the one I'd taken with Vivian at the department store.

"Would you like Him to come closer?" I asked.

"Yes, I want Him to come closer."

Stephen invited Jesus to come closer and closer, and this continued until Jesus stood directly behind him with His hands resting upon his shoulders. As Stephen recognized where Jesus was, he openly wept. Then he shared how he felt completely loved and protected and knew everything would be OK. Aware of Jesus standing behind him, he said, "I know Jesus has my back."

This encounter with Jesus transformed Stephen. He was so affected by the encounter that he shared the activation with his entire congregation the following Sunday. From the pulpit, he then helped them step into where God was for each of them as well.

Again, the key was to ask God *Where are You for me right now?* and then explore that space with further questions. While this isn't a discourse on the techniques of leading people into their God spaces, it is an encouragement for you to understand that you can do this. When you discover where God is for you at any moment, you'll become sure of His love for you, and you'll quickly learn how much you really are His happy, happy place.

ATHEISTS AND AGNOSTICS HAVE A GOD SPACE TOO

In the preceding stories we've seen a prodigal come home to Jesus, a pastor feel loved and protected by Jesus, and an entire congregation engage with Jesus in their God space. So Christians can all recognize where God is for them. But Dr. Divett's research went further than just believers. Her research established that *all* people have a God space. This reality isn't just for Christians alone. As the prophecy in Joel 2:28, fulfilled at Pentecost and quoted by Peter in Acts 2:17, states, "In the last days, God says, 'I will pour out my Spirit on *all people*'" (emphasis mine). "All people" includes atheists, agnostics, and even those of other faiths. Everyone has the Spirit poured out on them, therefore, all people have a God space!

Dr. Divett theorized and then established through meticulous research that *every* human being has a God space. But her research did find one basic difference between believers and pre-believers. She discovered pre-believers were not aware of God *within* themselves; they generally identified a place *outside* themselves. In comparison, Christians often, but not always, identified a place within.

It's exciting to think about the idea that all human beings have a space where they can identify where God is for them. It's a powerful concept to share with an agnostic or atheist if they're open to the idea. In my own adventures with God, I've also found that pre-believers encounter God outside themselves. Since gaining a basic understanding of God spaces, I've shared the concept with many others, always as prompted by the Holy Spirit. In my experience, every person encounters "something" (or I would say "a someone") they can't explain. These are often profound encounters that leave them without a doubt that something exists beyond themselves. They catch that they, too, are God's happy place, where He would like to be.

Let me share a few more personal testimonies to further establish this idea.

GOD IS GOOD STORY: THE NOSE THAT COULD NOT SMELL

This *God Is Good Story* is from my early days of praying for people as I went about my day. It involves the owner of the same hair salon I mentioned earlier—a woman I'll call Angela.

Angela said she'd lost her sense of smell. When I offered to pray, she explained she was an atheist and grinned wryly, saying, "Give it your best shot."

Well, I did give it my best shot regardless of the intimidation I felt. It was the end of the evening, and about ten hairdressers lined up to watch. Filled with fear and embarrassment, I prayed. I felt nothing as I prayed, Angela felt nothing, and she continued to smell . . . nothing!

I left feeling like a complete failure.

Once home, I had a good ole pity party and was ready to give up. However, my husband simply said to me, "This is merely one part of her journey," and on that small piece of encouragement, I continued praying for others as prompted by the Holy Spirit during my days.

Little did I know that God actually *had* restored Angela's sense of smell, but it was after I left. And it was six months before I discovered that. When I heard her news, I was in a state of shock. She said she would run around the salon and say to her employees, "I can smell that. Can you smell that? Oh, my gosh, I can smell that!" Suffice to say, I was glad I'd not given up praying for strangers throughout my days. But the story I want to share tells of another encounter Angela had with our loving God.

Now, even though God healed her, Angela continued to claim she didn't believe in Him. In response to her declarations of atheism, I offered to help her locate her God space so she could experience God for herself. After explaining what it was about, we sat down, and I gently led her to a place where she encountered great peace. She said God was like a warm, soft, fluffy orange blanket that wrapped around her shoulders.

"How does that feel? What is that like for you right now?" I asked.

"I feel warm, protected, comforted, and at complete peace."

Angela had found where God was for her, had discovered her God space. God prompted me to pray for her, to help her discover where God was for her in that moment, because of His deep desire for her to know how much He cared. He wanted her to appreciate that He was real, there, loving her, delighting in all that she was. He was wrapping her in His protective embrace, where there was comfort and loving peace. He was letting her know He was real. He saw her, He heard her, and she was His happy place.

I encouraged Angela some more, explaining she could go back to that place anytime she pleased. God was always available and happy for her to come. I explained she had encountered the One who loved her unreservedly, that she was His happy place.

But Angela isn't the only atheist who found their God space. The most powerful encounter I've seen involves an atheist in the schoolyard at morning drop-off.

GOD IS GOOD STORY: AN ATHEIST FINDS PEACE IN HER GOD SPACE

One morning at school drop-off, a fellow school mom encountered God's peace profoundly in her own God space. While a self-declared atheist, she had a genuine affection for me. We studied together at university and reconnected when our children enrolled in the same school. I have always really liked her. She was and remains a passionate, intelligent, kind person who fiercely loves her family. Let's call her Charlotte.

A few years before, as a committed atheist, Charlotte tried to stop all religious education in our state school. For her, it was a matter of principle. She passionately extolled her views on why religious education had no place in our state school system and actively tried to have it removed. After listening to her about her stance one morning, I gently let her know I was a Christian and said I disagreed.

She responded with grace. "You know what? I respect you. I love you, and I see you," she said.

We agreed to disagree and continued to encourage each other as parents of young children at the same school. Even so, I was cautious not to engage in any religious debate. To this day I strongly believe we don't win arguments by attacking another's views. I hold that we must refuse to be offended and rather meet people where they are. The Holy Spirit is superb at His job, and so through love, I allow space for a journey of discovery in each person I encounter.

On this particular morning, Charlotte was deeply distressed about her daughter. Platitudes like "It's going to be OK" weren't going to be enough. She was so upset that she was physically shaking, and as I spoke with her, she burst into tears.

I stood and listened to her mother's heart and all the complaints that weighed so heavily, and as I did, I felt the whisper of the Holy Spirit to offer to pray.

I hesitated. *You know she's an atheist, don't You?* But feeling His insistence, I offered her prayer. "Hey, I know you're an atheist. I know you don't believe in God. You also know I'm a Christian. So I'm going to offer . . . Can I pray for you?"

"You know what?" she said. "Give it your best shot. Yes!"

So I did. As I prayed, Charlotte cried some more and, feeling prompted by the Holy Spirit to talk to her about God spaces, I explained how we can all tangibly feel God's comfort and love. Then I briefly ran her through the concept of God spaces, together with the scientific research, including how it established that even atheists can access where God is for them at any moment.

"Would you be OK if I helped you find this space for yourself?" I asked.

She agreed, so I briefly took her through the protocol to help her find where God was for her. And as I did, she completely calmed down.

"Oh, I feel so peaceful," she said.

"Where is He for you right now?" I asked. "How is He making you feel?"

"I feel completely and utterly at peace, and I know that it's all going to be OK."

After a few moments, I explained she could go back to that place at any time. She was welcome there, regardless of her beliefs.

"I wish I could have a faith like yours," Charlotte responded.

I looked at her and said, "Hey, you can. It's just a decision." I then grinned and said, a little cheekily, "You may not believe in God, but He believes in you."

My beautiful passionate friend was God's happy place. She was His heart's desire. He was there for her in the moment of distress, and He was inviting her into a deeper relationship with Him.

Years later, Charlotte shared how the child we prayed about and for (now a teenager) was exploring Christianity even though she was being raised in an atheist home. Her beautiful daughter was actively seeking God and exploring the Christian faith.

Interesting! Neither Charlotte nor I could overlook the "coincidence."

Many Christians might criticize me for not entering a theological debate with my friend. Let me reiterate this point: We do not win by arguing with people. Rather, we "win" by allowing them to discover God for themselves—the God who loves them so well. We might lead the way by providing an encounter and allow them to experience Jesus. We let them feel how much He adores them. That experience becomes indisputable because they experience Him for themselves. It's *their* story that rests beyond the laws of logic that will often win them to Christ. We lead them there, and the Holy Spirit does the rest. Again, He does His job well! And Paul puts it so well: "Until then, there are three things that remain: faith, hope, and love—*yet love surpasses them all*. So above all else, let love be the beautiful prize for which you run" (1 Corinthians 13:13 TPT, emphasis added).

Love always wins, so let's share the prize with others and allow them to taste and see for themselves that God is good! Just like you, they are His happy place, and He's calling them all home. Of course, there's a time and place for intellectual debate, but first we must gauge where people are in their journey. Check in with the Holy Spirit about what to do next—go to *your* God space to see. If they're interested in theological debate, and they're "good soil," (receptive, not merely argumentative) provide them with some books, invite them into a discussion, take them to an Alpha course, read the Bible with them—do something. But remember, salvation is the work of the Holy Spirit, for "no one can say, 'Jesus is Lord,' except by the Holy Spirit" (1 Corinthians 12:3).

THE POWER OF GOD SPACES

Understanding that God created us all for a relationship with Him makes it logical that He would hardwire us to know Him for ourselves. It makes sense that we can all become aware of Him through understanding and finding our God space. And we can all empower those we love by helping them find where He is for them too! But even more powerfully, we can introduce Him to the world while understanding that each and every person we equip to find their God space is being invited into an understanding that *they* are God's happy place too —just like you.

QUESTIONS TO CONTEMPLATE

1. When in your past can you look back and recognize you encountered God? This could be through a person or directly for yourself in what you might now recognize as your God space. What was that like for you? Explore and journal the memories.
2. When have you been aware of God on the inside of you? What was that like? Go back to the memory or the place you identify and ask God to show you something more. If you don't recall a time, ask God to help you become aware of His indwelling presence in your life. Journal what you discover.
3. When have you been aware of God external to you? What was that like? What did He show you or tell you? But if you've never been aware of God external to you, ask Him where He is in your environment. Journal your impressions. Remember, God is in us, and we are in Him, so believers can experience the reality of both internal and external God spaces in their lives.

RESPONSE TO THE REVELATION

- **Action Step 1**: Each day this week, take some time to be still. Quieten your soul and ask, *God, where are You for me right now?* What do you see, hear, feel, know? Continue asking questions about the place where you sense God is for

you. Is He inside you, outside you, above you, below you? Journal what you discover as you seek Him.
- **Action Step 2:** Think of someone you can share this God space insight with, and then make time to do it. As we practice sharing the science, Scriptures, and testimonies, we'll become proficient and able to share it with anyone as we go about our day if prompted by the Holy Spirit. Ask God to give you opportunities to share what you've learned with people who don't yet know Jesus Christ as Lord and stop for anyone He highlights through your day.

LET'S PRAY

Father, I delight at the thought that I have a God space I can be aware of at any point in my day. Thank You for creating that space for me to encounter You whenever I please. I ask that You help me become more aware of Your presence as I seek You in my God space, and help me share this place with others. Thank You that You've created me to encounter You and encounter You I will as I seek You in my days. Thank You that Your Spirit has been poured forth upon all human beings so that all might come to know of Your goodness, kindness, and glory. In Jesus' mighty name I pray, amen.

7

PRESENT TO GOD

*Don't you realize that together you have become
God's inner sanctuary and that the Spirit of God
makes his permanent home in you?*
1 Corinthians 3:16 TPT

ONE OF THE greatest challenges we face in this modern world is distraction. With our faces turned to our screens, loved ones can be right by our side and yet we're not present to them in any meaningful way. They're there with us, but are we really *there* with them?

Understanding that we have a God space gives us the confidence to know we can all experience God for ourselves. We can all "turn to see where God is for me." But even if you feel you can't do this, you are still *with* Him. We simply can't be anywhere where God is not. We are His dwelling place and are therefore incapable of escaping Him. He is always "there," everywhere—in, around, and with us. Remaining ignorant of this truth might mean we fail to engage Him throughout our days, but our failure to do so doesn't negate the truth that He is there—*with us, everywhere, always.*

Ponder King David's insights in Psalm 139:7–10: "Where can I go from your Spirit? Where can I flee from your presence? If I go up to the heavens, you are there. If I make my bed in the depths, you are there. If I rise on the wings of the dawn, if I settle on the far side of the sea, even there your hand will guide me, your right hand will hold me fast."

Regardless of whether we're aware of God's presence, truth is truth. He's always with us, and He's always present to us. Engaging Him in our God space is great. However, life becomes far richer if we accept that God adores us and is ever present to us *everywhere* we go. He wants to do life *with* us, and we can learn to be ever-present to Him. Yet the sad reality is that so often we're not really present to Him. Just as so often we're not really present to those around us when we're on our phones.

Think of those times you were so caught up on your device that you missed a comment from your friend, spouse, or child. You might have been physically present *with* them, but you weren't present *to* them. Your awareness of them had simply left the room. We too-often treat God the same way. *He* is always aware of us and desires time with us. *He* wants to have conversations and discussions with us. *He* wants to engage us and is waiting for us to engage with Him. *He* is *always* by our side, but are we always aware of Him? Do we even notice Him at all?

The question to ask is not whether God is with us but why we sometimes believe He's not. Intellectual assent of the truth reflected in Psalm 139 isn't satisfying. We must have more. Imagine that you intellectually appreciate that you're married to your spouse but you never engage in any genuine interaction. Consider reading about your spouse in a book while he or she is by your side. In the same way we can read *about* God in the Bible, without recognizing He's in the room. If failing to be present in a relationship will damage it in the natural, why would we think it any different in our relationship with God? God is always "in the room" with us, but are we in the room with God?

I know sometimes I'm not. But why would that be? Because the awareness of the truth that God is there wavers. So the question to ask is whether we can become more aware of God's abiding presence, beyond being at church or during times of soaking, worship, or Bible reading. Well, I'm happy to say, yes, we can—by learning to be present to God.

WE LEARN TO LEAN IN

To grasp the idea of being present to God, imagine you're visiting with a friend in a bustling café. There's a lot of noise. The coffee machine is steaming, the door to the street opens and closes, people are talking around you, a child is chatting, a baby is crying. The hustle and bustle is loud and distracting. How do you hear your friend over all this?

Well, you listen with intent. You might turn your head or incline your ear to help you hear with clarity. To concentrate better on your friend's voice, you might lean in close. You learn to block out external noises and zone into your friend's presence. You watch their face and their movements. You stay focused, avoiding distractions. And out of politeness, you don't look at your phone, get up, walk away, change the topic, or talk over your friend with your own agenda. Instead, you sit still and listen as they speak. Even pauses and silence can communicate something to us.

We've all developed the skill to focus and ignore external distractions. We know how to shut out irrelevant noise as we listen to the one we want to hear. We learn how to become present to the person we're sitting with and hear what they have to say. They're *present* to us, and we're *present* to them. For some with heightened sensitivities, it might be more difficult, but as a general rule, we all develop this ability during our childhood. It takes practice, but we get there in the end. With growth, we refine the skill to listen intently to one another, and we learn to disregard the external world.

By extension, we learn to do the same with God. As we make time to be *with* Him—as we sit, listen, and lean into His voice—we become present *to* Him. There's an intentionality as we shut out the noise regardless of where we are. We can hear Him anywhere and everywhere, but in this chapter we're exploring the idea of spending time with Him alone. Yes, we can then take what we learn and be with Him throughout our days, but first we prioritize Him and spend time alone with the One we love.

This time I speak of is a regular time of being still and present with God. It's a quiet time when we turn off our phones, computers, radios, and televisions. We choose to focus on God. Music might help, but if not, we choose quiet. With distractions removed, we focus our thoughts and attention on Him. We might choose to read the Bible, and we might choose not to. Either way, we sit and are quiet with God.

I can guarantee you that in these moments of being present to God, He will be there. Well, He's already there, so perhaps it's more accurate to say you develop your awareness of Him. He might visit like my father did as I played my harp—silent, entering quietly, just to be with you. On a conscious level, we might not even be fully aware of Him, but having taught this long enough, I know beyond a doubt that He's there. Regardless of whether you think it's having any impact, setting aside time with God in this way will make a profound difference in your life.

Several years ago, I taught this process to a highly prophetic friend. Extraordinary miracles have happened throughout her life, and she recognizes and responds to God's voice well. She committed to try being present to God at a minimum of five minutes a day.

After a week or two, she said to me, "Oh, it doesn't work. I'm lying there and I don't feel Him, see Him, or hear Him."

"Tell me, what else is happening in your life?" I asked.

"Well, my husband says I'm more pleasant to be around. The house is calmer, and our home is more peaceful."

Her response told me all I needed to know. She'd been with God, and there was evidence of a tangible manifestation in her everyday life. The atmosphere in her home changed, and it was impacting her family and the way she coped with everyday challenges.

Regardless of whether you hear, see, feel, or know God when you practice being present to God, you can know beyond a doubt that He *is* there and His presence *will* impact you. Being present is merely our becoming aware of this truth. Do it for a while and ask others close to you if they notice a difference. They will, both in you and around you.

Imagine God is at a coffee shop with you and you're leaning in to hear. Spend that time being still with Him and watch Him go to work. I promise, as you lean in, you'll encounter a God who loves to spend time with you. I can also promise that the Holy Spirit loves it when we choose to stop and be still. It's as if we have the Trinity's attention. They all get excited. You can hear the breathlessness around the Trinity table: *Oh look. They're sitting with Us. Quick! Let's spend some time with them! Wow! They're inclining their ears. Let's tell them how much We love them.* Father God, Jesus Christ, and the Holy Spirit are always there with us, but They get excited when *you* become present to *Them*.

Again, I like to call practicing God's presence "soaking." That's because it's all about becoming saturated with God in such a way that we drip everywhere we go. But whatever the terminology we use, it's simply you learning to be present to Him. This is how we learn to be still and know that He is God.

As we become more aware of God in our quiet times, we'll see Him in everything we do and everywhere we go. It can be a bit like Moses and the burning bush. We're more aware of Him with us, and we'll know when to turn and look to see (like Moses) and to listen to what He will say to us (like Habakkuk). We recognize His presence, His nudging, as He speaks to us as we go about our day. Through this interaction, it becomes a "both/and" proposition, rather than an "either/or." It's *both* being still with Him at allocated times *and* being with Him as we go about our day, rather than one or the other.

From this place of being present to God, of soaking in His presence, you come to really *know* Him. And to truly know Him is to know of His goodness. It serves you well to always remember Moses when he asked to see God's glory. What did God choose to show of His glory? He said, "I will cause all my goodness to pass in front of you" (Exodus 33:19). This is fascinating given how in Romans 2:4 (NKJV) Paul tells us that it's God's goodness that leads people to repentance. It's His goodness (His kindness in the New International Version of the Bible) that draws people into a place of *wanting* to know Him. And it's these qualities that draw us into a place of wanting to know Him better as well.

PRESENT TO GOD

WHEN WE'RE AWARE OF HIM THROUGHOUT OUR DAYS

As we spend this time "soaking" in God's presence, we start to transform into His image, or dare I say, into more of who we truly are in Him. We're face-to-face with our creator, and from glory to glory we grow. We become what we behold (2 Corinthians 3:18). Time luxuriating in His extravagant love causes us to see others through His lens of love, and we see situations, places, cities, and people through His framework of reconciliation. With a solution focus, we also see the world as it is—it's getting brighter, for there is no end to His glory.

Remember, "In the beginning was the Word, and the Word was with God" (John 1:1). Jesus (the Word) is face-to-face with God (John 1:2 TPT). We are in Jesus (John 14:20) and so we are face-to-face with God as well. We rest within Jesus Christ through whose eyes we gaze and absorb the Father's love. As we become more aware of this truth, so we become more aware of God. We soak in His radiant glory, and as shining ones we go forth into the world transformed by His gaze of love.

This time spent simply *being* with God helps us be more aware of His presence throughout our days. There is a leaking of kingdom realities through us into the world. We slosh with the flowing fountains of water that Jesus references in John 4:14: "The water I give them will become in them a spring of water welling up to eternal life." This then makes its way into everything we do. We "leak" the goodness of God as He draws others to Himself, through us.

Let me explain through a story.

GOD IS GOOD STORY: AND HE WAS SEEN (PART 1)

One night I was purchasing a few grocery items in a little store. Located across the road from my children's elite dance school, the store often hired older students in their final year of training. As a young man I'll call William waited on me, I became aware of God's presence and felt a prompting to pray. I knew he was in his final year of training from the school across the road, and I mentioned my unction to pray and asked him if I could.

He responded immediately "Yes, absolutely."

Regardless of familiar nerves, I took his hand in mine and prayed.

I want to stop here for a moment. Let's pull back the curtain. Many believe I don't feel fear. They claim I'm bold and an extrovert, and therefore I find it easy to stop for the one in this way. Only one of those statements is true. Yes, I'm bold, but I feel fear nearly every time I stop to pray for someone. By nature, I'm a highly sensitive personality type, and I err on the side of introversion. On this occasion, I felt a strong sense of fear, which included a fear for my children. They also trained at the dance facility, and a complaint about me could fare very badly for them. I had to choose to step through that fear, and I was very glad I did.

Feeling God's presence, I knew He wanted me to call in William's destiny. I sensed William hadn't felt seen for all the years he'd trained—and it *had* been years! I also knew he not only *felt* this way, but that those in charge had, in fact, *overlooked* him. He was completely unseen.

So in response to my discernment, aware of God's presence, I prayed and called William into the light, declaring it was time for him to be seen and for the doors of his destiny to finally open in the name of Jesus Christ. I looked at him, briefly stopping to explain what I felt and what I'd prayed for. It was important for me to unpack it for him so he could understand. He focused on me intently, then told me that was *exactly* how he felt. The establishment and auditioning bodies had never seen him. Constantly overlooked, he felt and was completely unseen.

"William" asked me my name, and I gave him my first name. Now, I usually provide my first name before I pray. It's a matter of courtesy. And then the people I pray for usually give me their name so I can address them appropriately. But this young man pushed a little and asked for my surname too. I was hesitant, but it seemed important for him to know who I was, so I told him. He thanked me and looked like he'd physically felt something—the presence of God as I prayed. I didn't ask if he had, still cautious with so much to lose for my children.

He stared at me. "Thank you, Beth Kennedy."

I smiled. "You are so very welcome!"

I thought that was all I needed to do, but as I went to leave the store, an urgent boldness came over me. It was as if I suddenly knew that I knew it really *was* time for him to be seen. Exactly as I had prayed, it was his time. Aware of God's presence, with a sudden sassy attitude engulfing my being, I grew incensed about how he had remained unseen. I had a visceral reaction and thought *This is not OK!* as I *felt* God's heart of justice for him in that instant.

Turning to God, I saw a picture flash across my imagination. I saw a ballet scene, an image of William as a king walking onto a stage. He walked the way royalty would, and as he walked, I saw a double door opening before him. The way dancers hold themselves is pure elegance in motion. With their shoulders held back and their head held high, they sweep their arms before them with dignity and grace. It evokes the sense of *Well, of course the doors opened, because this is who I am.*

I stopped in my tracks, looked at him, and said, "This is what I'm seeing for you." And although I felt silly, I acted out the scene in the middle of the store, explaining what I was doing as I went.

"Wow!" he said in awe after watching and listening.

"*This* is how it will be for you," I said with boldness. "You *will* walk, and the doors *will* open. No effort from you. There will be no need to push. You won't need to strive. You'll just walk it out like a king. The double doors will open."

I explained further that he *was* a king; he was royalty, a prince. I told him to imagine he was a prince, much like the roles he danced. As I spoke this, I stood as tall as I could and stepped forward, motioning with my arms as royalty would as they walked through open doors. When royalty does this, there's no effort on their behalf. Doors simply open for them. I acted this out for him, too, and then turned to look at him, feeling foolish but feisty all at once.

William looked encouraged and nodded with understanding.

Now, remember, as far as I know, he was a pre-believer.

I said defiantly, "I call it in Jesus' name. No effort, no striving. It will just happen, and I look forward to hearing all about it!"

A few weeks later, I was back in this store with a friend. We were having a cup of tea, and William was working. In my heart, I thought, *I don't want to ask him how it all went.* I felt it had all been a little strange and what I'd prayed had been rather far-fetched in the natural.

I briefly chatted with my friend, and as we were leaving, William stopped me. "Do you remember you prayed for me a few weeks ago? Well . . ."

I felt such joy rise inside me. "Oh, my gosh! You have an offer of a contract?" I said, grinning.

"I have!" he said with a grin of his own.

"I want to hug you!" I was so excited!

"You can hug me," he replied.

So I hugged him and said, "God is good. God is good!"

He looked at me and said, "He *is* good! He *is* good!"

William then explained that after I prayed for him, he received a contract offer from an overseas dance company. The company wanted him to start with them soon, but he wanted to finish his course. Writing to them with his desires, they agreed to wait so he could go early the following year.

I jumped with sheer delight and hugged him again. I had to go collect my son, but said I'd return. When I did, I learned William had auditioned for a British dance company touring in Australia. He originally auditioned for a couple of roles that would have given him a small amount of work here. He was unsuccessful. The auditioners completely overlooked him. However, after our prayer, the people responsible for the Australian auditions asked if they could put his name forward to the director.

Ever the performer, he paused for effect, then said, "The director contacted me! Personally!"

I gasped. This never happens in the dance world, and I was breathless with God's kindness. He continued to share more so-called coincidences. On speaking to the director, an offer for a permanent contract came from the very company who originally overlooked him. He was delighted, and I was too!

"These are *not* coincidences," I told him. "This is God moving on your behalf. They're God coincidences."

I explained that all I'd done was pray and then prophesy. Then I explained how prophecy is simply hearing God's heart for another and telling them what God says to share. I said I'd heard God's heart for him and had agreed with it through my prayer. It *was* his time to be seen.

William nodded, seeming to understand. We *both* knew it was an answer to prayer.

"Maybe you'll come see me dance someday," he said.

"What a delight and a pure pleasure that would be," I replied.

I smiled all the way home for the sheer joy of seeing God express His love for another human being. The joy was tangible. It's a privilege to be involved in someone's journey. By being present to God as I went about my day, I'd been given the opportunity to partner with the one true God who saw this young ballet dancer, and it was a privilege to release his destiny. There's nothing better than being aware of God's presence, partnering with Him, and then witnessing people step into all they're called to do!

For William, I was the conduit of a loving God who saw him and loved him so much that He reached out, through me, to release His living waters. Jesus is the living waters that flows from my innermost being to the world (John 4:14). It was William's beginning, like it was for the woman at the well (John 4:4–42). I knew he would grow more in his understanding of God. God saw him and knew him and heard his deep heart cry. William was on his journey of discovery that he was God's happy place, and I knew this was just a first step for him to learn how to be present to God for himself.

BEING PRESENT, WE WILL SEE BEYOND OURSELVES

This story beautifully highlights how it's not through our performance that God releases us into our destiny. Nor is it through our performance that we can encounter God. God encounters us because He adores us. We are His happy place, and He wants us to become aware of Him—believer and pre-believer alike. William didn't yet *know* God for himself, and yet God reached out through me to kiss him into His purpose and heart's desire to dance. He had done nothing to deserve this attention. It was from *who* God *is*, rather than a response to William's good behavior. God is a loving Father. And as such, He provided the release for William to step into purpose and destiny. As He did so, God let him know He'd always been in his life. It just required me to show the way, to help him become more aware of God for himself.

Being present to God will allow you to taste and see God is good in so many ways. Our awareness of God increases as we go about our day while consciously being present to Him. In this way, we'll see Him everywhere. He'll whisper sweet nothings to us, while giving us assignments to bless others. As we lean in and are present to Him, the banks of our hearts will burst forth *with* Him. However, it's not what you've done nor even the time you've spent with Him that He rewards. We earn nothing from Him. Rather, it's because of *who* He is that He gives and helps us become aware of His presence. We then learn how to be aware of Him in our daily lives, and from the overflow, as we live present to Him, we impact others.

It's also important to recognize that we don't need to know who God is to be seen, heard, and known by Him. Even pre-believers can feel and recognize His attention. We can all become present to Him. God loved this young dancer, and He loves us too. We just need to turn to see—actively be present to Him. In practicing His presence, there will be a life exchange where you will catch the truth that He is everywhere and He adores you, for you are His happy place.

As we develop this awareness, we see Him in everything, everywhere. We come to know Him, and to know Him is to know His generosity. William continued to see provision flow, learning to recognize God's fingerprints in the processes of his life. His story continued to get better, and this first encounter led to more, then more, then even more. His awareness of God increased, and William tasted and saw of

God's goodness. Indeed, God got busy, and even showed off. Through it all, William began to recognize God's presence. He was learning to turn to see.

GOD IS A GOOD STORY: AND HE WAS SEEN (PART 2)

I saw William many times over the next few months. Each time he updated me with more amazing things that kept occurring in his life. It became such that every time I saw him, he had another God story to tell. He could see God's presence in everything he did.

As mentioned, soon after my first encounter with William, the director of a great British dance company contacted him to offer a job. The start date was a little too early and wouldn't have allowed him to complete his dance training and qualifications. We prayed for favor, and he wrote to the director, hoping to negotiate a later start date. The director offered a later start, but this new date was a little too late, so we prayed again, asking that the job would start just a little earlier and for the employment contract to come forth so it could be signed, sealed, and delivered.

A subsequent offer came with an earlier start date. Indeed, the dates were perfect. He had time to travel, and then time to find somewhere to live and settle in. It was perfect in all ways, but the contract wasn't forthcoming.

On a further visit, I asked about the delayed contract. It still hadn't arrived. I recalled a beautiful testimony about a contract not turning up for a friend's job, which arrived the day immediately after prayer. I told him the testimony and said, "Let's pray God does the same and the contract comes quickly!" Within days, the contract appeared with enough time to finish school, travel, and start the new job. Everything was exactly what William wanted.

Now, unbeknownst to him, I'd also asked God to cause a major Australian company to notice him and that he would have opportunities to shine. As mentioned, he'd previously shared with me how the Australian hierarchy seemed to overlook him, so I had cheekily asked God for an Aussie revealing.

I saw William again at a later date. He looked tired, but happy. With extreme joy he said the director of the top Australian company had given him opportunities to dance with the touring company. The roles offered were unexpected but very welcome. He told me how the director had recognized particular gifts in him for a few roles and offered them. It was an answer to my private prayers—his chance to shine in the Aussie scene, and he did!

Delighted by this news, I sheepishly confessed that I'd been praying for him. I gently encouraged him to rest, and he allowed me to pray for a deep refreshing as he came into this current season of exams and finalization of his education. God was making Himself known in his life in radical and unexpected ways.

Unexpectedly, I saw William yet again, and to my absolute delight he told me yet another great Australian company had offered him a contract, as had a major New Zealand one too. These offers were all coming very late according to industry standards. Our prayers were being answered even more than I'd dared to hope or believe for.

"You've got so many offers on the table. What are you going to do?" I asked him.

"I'm still going to the UK. It feels right in my heart."

"I'm so pleased for you," I said. "When God opened those doors, He really opened those doors!"

He laughed, agreeing with me.

"You're on a beautiful, wonderful journey, and a very good God loves you," I told him.

William thought for a moment, then said, "I don't know what that looks like. I don't have a grid for all of this."

"It looks like what you've been experiencing a God who sees you, loves you, and is inviting you into a relationship with Him. You're learning to recognize His presence in all you do."

I gently explained that if he wasn't ready to ask Jesus into his life that day, all he had to do was say, "Jesus, I want you in my life. I open my heart to you." I then said that in faith, he could just step in. In that way he would become even more present to God than he was before.

I explained it was OK for him not to be too sure. It was a journey of discovery. God was pursuing him. All he needed to do was pray, even as a pre-believer, ask for God's guidance about anything, and God would respond. I explained he would feel a quiet assurance resting upon the right decisions and choices. I was gently teaching him how to be aware of God's presence and how to be present to Him. He was God's happy place, and God wanted only what was best for him.

"One way to know is that you will be at peace with the decision. It will sit right in your heart," I said, paraphrasing Colossians 3:15. "As a Christian, I believe I know what happened to you. I know who asked me to pray for you on that first occasion. And I know this is your first time encountering Him with an understanding of what's actually happening. I'm happy to answer your questions to the best of my ability, but this is your journey, and no one could or should force the issue."

Then I gave William a few testimonies about other people who, after three or four years of me walking with them, finally said yes to Jesus.

"You've experienced how much God loves you," I said. "You know He's real, and you know He cares. It's now a beautiful dance of coming together, knowing and loving each other."

As we know, a journey with God isn't a single encounter. We're living out our salvation. It's a life journey—a continuous going deeper into a relationship with a loving God. And to go deeper requires us to be present to God. It's going in and out, just as Jesus said when He talked about being the door (John 10:9). Being known by God is a given, but it's also knowing God for ourselves. It's learning to be present with Him.

I trust William's encounters with our loving Father will continue. It's my hope that he reaches out to God for himself. I also hope he can establish a grid for what happened to him as he comes to know that God loves and adores him, just as he is, for he is also God's happy place.

What I do know is that God set His sights upon him, but not because he checked all the boxes and had been a good Christian. God encountered him because He is the God who sees. He's a God who loves. He's a God who is present to all of us, whether saved or unsaved. God is a loving Father who constantly draws all of humankind to Himself, wanting our response to be yes, constantly calling us to be present to Him.

CATCHING GOD'S HEART

As we are present to God, we'll become more aware of Him in whatever we do, and it will become second nature to introduce Him to others. Spending time with God helps us recognize His voice. In the space of quiet time, we learn His ways, and we catch His heart for ourselves and for those all around us. Some call this "the secret place"; others call it "practicing His presence." Once more, I like to call it "soaking," and of course, Dr. Divett calls this place of awareness our God space. Whatever we might call it, by intentionally spending time with God, remaining focused and aware, we'll become more present to Him.

This awareness will grow, and it will be natural to include Him in our conversations. We're constantly hanging out with a generous, kindhearted God who performs miracles, signs, and wonders everywhere we go. That's because where we are, He is too. Being *with* God is being with the best person you could imagine—and then some. And the great thing is He feels the same way about you! He adores His time with you, and just likes to hang, because *you* are His happy place.

QUESTIONS TO CONTEMPLATE

1. Where do you find it easiest to be aware of God's presence? Why do you think that is? Journal your insights.
2. Now that you've been on this journey for a while, think about the times you've had an increased awareness of God's presence. Where was it and when? What made you more aware in those moments? Think of ways you could become

PRESENT TO GOD

more aware throughout your days, then journal what comes to mind.

3. Do you have places you can put up sticky notes to remind yourself to be aware of God's presence? Where are those places? What other methods could you use to help remind you that God is with you? Ask God what He thinks you can do to increase your awareness of Him throughout your days. Journal your thoughts, insights, and God's suggestions and consider adopting some of the ideas. *Note:* As you commit to being more conscious of God with you everywhere you go, your awareness will grow. As this occurs you can practice asking Him questions, which will increase your awareness even more. Ask Him if there's somewhere He'd like to go, or something He'd like to do, or someone He'd like you to speak to. If you have work outside the home, as you journey there ask Him, *Which way would You like me to get to work today? What's on Your agenda for my day?*

RESPONSE TO THE REVELATION

- **Action Step 1:** Write Psalm 139:7–10 in your journal, but in place of the words *I* and *me*, write your name. Then read it aloud to yourself. Journal what you see, hear, feel, sense, and know as you hear these words spoken over you.
- **Action Step 2:** Now read the Scripture you've written with your name into a recording device, like your smartphone. Play the recording back to yourself every day for a week. Listen quietly, allowing it to permeate your being. After listening to the recording, sit still and be present to God. Have a cup of tea or coffee and practice His presence. Start your time by exploring where God is for you, identifying your God space, and from there focusing on Him. Ponder a favorite Scripture if it helps. I like to think of the woman at

the well in John 4, or Mary sitting at the feet of Jesus in Luke 10:38–42. Sit quietly, listen, and allow Him to minister to you in quietness. If you find your attention drifting, focus back on where God is for you and continue. Journal what you see, hear, feel, taste, smell, and know as you are present to God. Each day journal how your awareness of God increases.

LET'S PRAY

Father, thank You for being ever present with me. And not only present with me but within me. Thank You that I can't escape You, that You are always there, with me, in all I do. I'm sorry for when I've failed to notice You. Please forgive me and help me become more present to You. Help me lean in and hear Your voice through my nights and days. Help me see beyond myself, to You and through You to others too. In Jesus' mighty name I pray, amen.

8

CHANGED IN HIS PRESENCE, CHOSEN FOR HIS PURPOSE

John answered them all, "I baptize you with water. But one who is more powerful than I will come, the straps of whose sandals I am not worthy to untie. He will baptize with the Holy Spirit and fire."
Luke 3:16–17

AS WE ALLOW Jesus to permeate our being, we're permanently changed. We become saturated in His substance and carry His presence out to the world. Unknowingly, we imbue atmospheres with His goodness, changing the world according to His design merely because we're there, hosting Him as we go. We simply cannot spend time in His presence without being changed. And as we change we are chosen for His purpose, a purpose He had for us before time even began.

BAPTISMS

My journey in Jesus Christ has involved two water baptisms. Soon after giving my heart to Jesus, I was "sprinkled" in front of family and friends. The church tradition I was a part of at the time sprinkled drops of water on people's heads for baptism in comparison to submerging a person in water, as is the practice of other church traditions. It was a special day, and as I left the church, I hoped others would follow me into a faith in Jesus.

A few years later I had a growing desire to be rebaptized, submerged. I had read and learned more, and after some consideration, my husband, Andrew, and I went to be baptized together in a local swimming pool. Only a few believers came this time, and photos taken immediately before and after reveal a light on our faces as we emerged from the water. The light wasn't there before we went under, but it was there immediately after. We explored all other plausible explanations and eventually concluded it was heaven's light. We've baptized many people since, and at each baptism we take a before and after photo. The same light rests upon every face. It's a mystery—but a delight to behold.

Other baptisms ensued. A baptism in the Spirit, evidenced by the gift of tongues, came, but so did others where something mysterious occurred. Oftentimes, I didn't know what, for although I left knowing I'd profoundly changed from within, I never quite knew to what effect. I'm sure there have been others, ones I'm completely unaware of until someone makes a comment later.

Years after my "sprinkling," as I became imbued with God's love, my desire to be immersed fully in God's presence grew. My awareness of Him increased exponentially, until one day I was so aware of Him and the reality of God in my life that I felt at one with John 17:15–16: "My prayer is not that you take them out of the world but that you protect them from the evil one. They are not of the world, even as I am not of it." I was *in* the world, but I was not *of* it.

Those days, as I walked our neighborhood streets pushing my son's stroller and dropping my daughter off at school, I was acutely aware of the presence of God. I felt otherworldly, one foot placed firmly in the eternal realm beyond. My awareness of Jesus was so real—and the needs and desires of the world, by comparison, so dim—I felt I didn't belong here. And yet the flow of His love for those around me caused me to burn with a desire to share Him wherever I went.

As this increased, I had what felt like trysts with my beloved God. I couldn't wait to be with Him, to know Him, to see Him. I was being progressively changed in His presence. Because of my intense desire to develop the gift of healing and prophecy, I'd been stopping for the one, and as I did, I learned the sound of my Lord's voice as I listened and responded in obedience. An abandoned stance drove me to see His reality realized everywhere I went, and as I pursued His gifts, a subtle shift occurred. I desired one thing more than anything else: to be with my Lord Jesus. It was all about Him, His ways, His desires, and His heart. And in return, He showed me how delighted He was with me, how I was His happy place.

With my world turning upside down, whenever I could I retreated into the secret place. I listened and read everything to grow as much as possible. My appetite to learn was unquenchable. In faith, I would simply quieten my soul to be with Him. I soon knew I was being changed day by day.

Every nap my son took, I would "soak" in the Lord. Lying down in the presence of God, just as Samuel did, I said, *Speak, Lord, for your servant is listening*. My awareness of God was so acute, my obedience so radical, that it rattled my marriage. My husband affirmed that our home felt better after I'd spent time with the Lord, and he agreed I was more loving and that life was sweeter. But he felt jealous of the lover of my soul. (Eventually, Andrew, too, went on a journey such that all jealousy fell away.)

Past issues in my world were being stripped back and poor behavior patterns were rapidly addressed as the Holy Spirit gently reprimanded me with a burning in my heart. With each day, He called me deeper into my truest identity: *This is not who you are, My Beth. Don't do that.* He would woo me with His love and words. The refining fire was purging me, and I continued to change daily in His presence. He chose me for Himself, and in Him I found my purpose. And it was His purpose all along. The stirrings were insistent, passionate, and intense, and they required everything of me. He wooed, and I submitted myself willingly to the cleansing fire blazing in my soul.

Now, don't get me wrong, I wasn't perfect, and many times I wanted to retreat. The laying down of past and present hurts was difficult. Stripped back raw, I wanted to run. But it was not from His gaze that I wished to flee. Rather, I desired an escape from the pain being revealed, the process He required of me to choose His ways rather than my own. I fought the desire to flee from others too—the many who judged, who didn't understand. I also wanted to flee what it might ultimately cost in my world—the cost to myself, but more so, the cost to my children, my family, my life.

As these days progressed, I realized more was happening around me without my conscious input. I came to understand I was dripping the goodness of God just by being in a room. People noticed something different about me, and they'd mention what they felt and saw. Many people spoke of a light in my face or a light emanating from within. Later, Andrew received the same type of comments about himself, for as I said earlier, he, too, went on a journey. People said they could feel a peace and tangible love. A deep, indescribable joy was mine, yet simultaneously, the refining continued as I entered and reentered the Holy of Holies with Jesus.

I can only describe that when I spent time deep in the presence of God, a mystical exchange seemed to occur. I felt like a dry sponge going in and would come out dripping with His tangible presence. Then I would go out and drip His essence. With each soaking, a baptism took place, saturating me more deeply, more thoroughly. I also discovered a deeper layer of my truest self. Parts of me fell away, parts that weren't truly *me*, and I became certain God really had chosen *me* for His purpose. Discovering how deeply He loved me, my "Amen" naturally followed His yes (2 Corinthians 1:20), and it was here in His presence that I learned I truly was His happy place.

I share this to encourage you. You *will* change in His presence, and as you do, He *will* choose you for His purpose. But, I must add, it's not the time in His presence that somehow "qualifies" you, for in Jesus you're already qualified. Rather, it's in His presence that you'll discover He chose you before time as He stretched His arms wide on the cross and said (paraphrasing), "Yes, I choose them!" From the start, He said, "I pick you, for Myself, and for My purposes." And in the presence of God, you learn that His purpose for you was your deep desired purpose all along. Saint Augustine put it so beautifully: "You have made us for yourself, O Lord, and our heart is restless until it rests in you."

We'll always remain restless until we sink into God's presence. Once sunken, in that submerged place, we find deep joy, and to our sheer delight and surprise we discover our purpose was always within us, where it lay within Him.

LIKE SUNKEN TREASURE, WE ARE SUBMERGED IN JESUS CHRIST

John the Baptist's words, describing *his* purpose in God, help point the way to our destiny deep in Jesus. He declares, "The one who sent me to baptize with water told me, 'The man on whom you see the Spirit come down and remain is the one who will baptize with the Holy Spirit'" (John 1:33).

Each of the four Gospels refers to John's role (Mark 1:8; Luke 3:16; Matthew 3:11; John 1:31). Sent to prepare the people's hearts, John proclaims the coming of the Messiah. With symbolic significance, he then dips them into water to show their readiness for the coming. In contrast, Jesus came to baptize us, or permanently submerge us, in the Holy Spirit and fire (Mark 1:8; Luke 3:16; Matthew 3:11).

Like treasures hidden in darkness (Isaiah 45:3), Jesus sinks us deep into His Spirit, baptizing us with fire and a passion to burn brightly for Him. As He does so, He sinks deep into us, and a symbiotic union forms as He invites us into an awareness of His presence—where we change, understanding we are His happy place, chosen before time as His bride, and drenched in His purposes.

In looking up the Greek Lexicon's explanation of the word *baptism*, we gain insight into our mysterious union in Jesus Christ. The New Testament authors used two words: *bapto* and *baptizo*. While conceptually alike, they're different in significant ways. The word *bapto* means "to be submerged temporarily into a solution." It's a *temporary* dipping—like what John did for his followers.

We can find an example in Luke 16:24, when a rich man calls out,

"Father Abraham, have pity on me and send Lazarus to dip [bapto] the tip of his finger in water and cool my tongue, because I am in agony in this fire."

In contrast, baptizo means "to be submerged permanently, continuously in a solution." It's a continuous soaking rather than a simple dipping—like what Jesus does for us in His Holy Spirit and fire. It also means "to dip repeatedly, to immerse, to submerge," like sunken treasure, surrounded, infiltrated by the very water into which it has sunk. And last, baptizo can also mean "to cleanse by dipping or submerging, to wash, to make clean with water, to wash oneself, bathe" or "to overwhelm."

While the word *baptizo* is a derivative of the word *bapto*, and is similar in meaning, the use of both words in writings contemporaneous to the writing of the New Testament Scriptures can help us understand their vernacular meaning in Jesus' time.[1]

"PICKLE" DEEP IN GOD'S PRESENCE

Imagine how the New Testament authors might have struggled to conceptualize what happened to them through the baptism of Jesus Christ at Pentecost (Acts 2:14–19). Just think of how they might have searched to find *the* exact words, to communicate the complexity of what took place through their baptism, their thorough soaking in the Holy Spirit.

Beautifully, a recipe dated to about 200 BC for pickled vegetables gives us insight into the different usage of the two words *bapto* and *baptizo*. This contemporaneous writing helps us catch the distinct meaning of the two words and gives us a hint of what the New Testament authors were trying to convey.

Written by a Greek poet and physician called Nicander, we learn that to make a pickled vegetable, the vegetable in question should first be "dipped" (bapto) into boiling water. He then states it should then be "baptized" (baptizo) into a vinegar solution—the substance that forms the pickling fluid.

While both are verbs, the first is a *temporary* immersion, a dipping, and the second is a *permanent soaking*, a "baptizing" that brings about permanent change. It's the second immersion that pickles the vegetable. In Nicander's words, the vegetable is "baptized" in vinegar. In the pickling (the full immersive soaking), the vegetable takes on the substance of vinegar. The absorption causes a permanent change to the vegetable fully immersed.[2]

So when John the Baptist says his baptism is inferior to the baptism of Jesus Christ, he's referencing his dipping compared to the impact of the permanent submersion, the baptizo, of Jesus Christ. John says, "I baptize you with water. But one who is more powerful than I will come, the straps of whose sandals I am not worthy to untie. He will baptize with the Holy Spirit and fire" (Luke 3:16–17).

In Acts 19:2–5, Paul finds disciples baptized only with the baptism of John the Baptist, and so Paul baptizes them in the name of Jesus and they receive the Holy Spirit. They are "baptized"—pickled, saturated, soaked, or permanently changed in the presence of the Holy Spirit. Their pickling changes them forevermore.

We see the outworking of this baptism, of Jesus Christ's baptizo, at Pentecost as the Holy Spirit and fire pour forth. Peter stands amid the chaos and says to all in attendance, "Repent and be baptized, every one of you, in the name of Jesus Christ for the forgiveness of your sins. And you will receive the gift of the Holy Spirit" (Acts 2:38). And Acts 2:41 says, "Those who accepted [Peter's] message were baptized, and about three thousand were added to their number that day."

Even Paul teaches how *he* was baptized, baptizo, "into Christ" in Galatians 3:27: "All of you who were baptized [baptizo] into Christ have clothed yourselves with Christ." Paul says Christ clothes and covers us. We are "hidden *with* Christ" (Colossians 3:3) and fully saturated. Covered, submerged, and saturated in the presence of Christ, we change in His presence, and we learn how we're chosen for His purpose. Like the vegetable pickled in vinegar, we're still us in form, yet we taste, smell, and drip with Christ. Just as the pickled onion tastes, smells, and drips with the vinegar, we take on the fragrance of Christ and carry it to the world. We taste of Him, and as we spend more time *with* Him, He permeates our very being, and our awareness of Him grows.

The more time we spend with God, the more He'll permeate our understanding of who He is and who we are in Him. We are "pickled" in Him, and this pickling changes us. And in this place we awaken to His choice. He chooses us for Himself and for His purposes. We say, *Pick me!* and He replies, *I already did. My purpose was always within you. It just took time soaking in me for you to find Me, and in finding Me, you found your true self! Now step fully into your purpose, which has been My purpose all along.* The pickling time in Him ultimately pickles us into His purposes too.

The onion tastes of vinegar; we taste of Jesus Christ. The onion drips in vinegar; we drip in Jesus Christ. As we submerge in Him, we will manifest elements of Him.

Let me explain a little more. As the onion pickles, the essence of the onion stays the same. It always is and always remains an onion, yet it undergoes a radical change through the submersion in the vinegar solution, such that it takes on a new form. It becomes a pickled onion. So, too, we transform into new creations. Old habits wash away, and true self becomes revealed.

Thinking of ourselves as the onion allows us to fully grasp that we are His good idea, His happy place. He wants us to be ourselves in the same way we want the onion to be an onion. He doesn't want us to disappear, just as we don't want the onion to disappear into the fluid and no longer be an onion. Rather, He wants us *fully* aware of Him as we live *in Him* and He lives *in us*. Together we make a great team. Together, we're unstoppable. It's Jesus Christ in us, Jesus Christ through us, and us in Jesus Christ. It's Jesus and you! You *are* changed in His presence, and in being so you transform for His purpose, which has been your truest, most joy-filled purpose all along.

Now, the battle around spending time with Him can be fierce. We're in an age of distraction when so many things compete for our attention. Our focus is where the place of fiercest resistance will come, but as mentioned before, spending time with God is never a waste of time. Choosing to "pickle in His presence" (spend time with Him) causes us to become more aware of the union that will never break. In that place, we become dangerous to the powers of darkness and incredibly effective agents for the kingdom of Light.

GET PICKLED IN HIS PRESENCE, AND YOU'LL BE PICKLED IN HIS PURPOSE

Time spent *with* God is an entry point while simultaneously being an endpoint. It's a pathway through which our awareness of Him (Father, Son, and Holy Spirit) expands so that we become ever more present to Him who is ever present to us. This has been His plan all along—relationship! But so, too, has been the family expansion plan. Both are His purpose for us all, for there's always room for more at the table of the Lord.

We change in His presence, and as we do, He chooses us for His purposes—or rather, we choose His purpose for ourselves. He loves us first, we learn how He adores us, and we love in return. Permeated in His presence, we change, and we desire what He desires. It becomes a win/win/win.

Now, again, as with many metaphors, hold this next one lightly. The explanation serves a purpose. We dwell in Him always, and He dwells in us, always, so strictly speaking we're already and always saturated with Him. To know that helps us to shift from a "lack mentality" into an "abiding mentality." The fullness of the Godhead is already in us, and we're already in them, but the example I give will help us all catch the power that we can "soak in the presence" of God. And like an onion that pickles in a pickling solution, we can become imbued with Him such that we drip Him wherever we go.

LIKE A SATURATED SPONGE, WE DRIP

Imagine a large bowl of water (Father, Son, and Holy Spirit). Above the bowl is a dry, parched sponge (us). We give our hearts to Christ, but like the sponge, we're dry, and we need to engage with the reality of Him. The truth is He's already within us, and He's all around us, but we have a limited awareness of Him. The worries of the world are upon our shoulders, and so we go to Him, dipping into the water. A little of the sponge becomes wet.

We spend a bit more time with Him, and we feel a little better. As we do, our true form as a soft spongy sponge will begin to take shape. But remember, if the sponge doesn't return to the water, it will dry out again—just as the cares of the world will dry us out too.

So we, the sponge, return to the bowl, and soak and soak and soak again. The more water we absorb, the fuller we become, until eventually we drip as we leave the bowl of water. The sponge is still a sponge, but it's a fully formed, saturated sponge, dripping with water wherever it goes. We can't help but leak with His essence, His living waters (John 4:14).

This occurred to the woman at the well in John 4. She spent time in the presence of Jesus and, fully saturated, she went forth. Her time with Him dramatically changed her. She realized He'd chosen her for His purpose, which was her purpose all along, and she evangelized an entire region. She was a saturated sponge, baptized in His living waters. Pickled in His presence, she drew in His fragrance, and through her transformation, an entire community came to Jesus Christ.

So you enter His presence and soak, and as you emerge, like the sponge, you drip. Sometimes you hug another sponge, and they take on more of their sponge shape too. You give them a drink from your source, but you must choose to go back and soak some more. Life becomes easier when we continuously go back to where God is and soak. We can choose to sit at the feet of Jesus, like Mary did in Luke 10:39, and simply behold Him until we flow with the essence of His living waters. Eventually, like the sponge, our awareness expands, and as it does we become fully submerged like a fat dripping sponge or a fully pickled onion. It's not a simple dip; it's a permanent submersion, a constant soaking, in Him.

Regardless of our conscious awareness, when we've been soaking in Him, we will drip as we go about our day. In this state, we might run into someone who's dry, feeling the weight of the world, and whether they're a believer or a pre-believer, as we speak life, they'll feel Jesus' in us, on us, and through us. We might not even mention His name, but we will leak and, just as many pre-believers have told me they did, they'll receive His life-giving presence.

Then we go back and soak some more, and we run into that same person. They receive more of His life-giving presence. They might say, "What is it about you? I always feel so much better around you. I feel accepted and loved when I'm with you. You're always so encouraging, full of hope."

It's you, but it's not you. It's the "pickling solution," because as a sponge, you're dripping everywhere you go. Eventually, many of them will seek what it is about you. They learn that the difference is Jesus Christ, and they might choose Him and learn to soak, too, becoming a dripping sponge. This has happened repeatedly in my walk with Jesus, and it *will* happen to you.

Sometimes we're just a "drippy sponge" affecting people on their journey to Christ. We might never see them again. Other times, we have the privilege of walking with them side by side and ultimately seeing them make that decision for Jesus. The joy is seeing others become "submerged sponges" who go, flow, and affect the world around *them*. Changed in God's presence, they're chosen for His purpose too!

We see this rhetorical question asked in Isaiah 66:8: "Can a country be born in a day or a nation be brought forth in a moment?" The answer of course is yes! Our response is so often, *But how, God?* Well, *this* is how we can ultimately "change a nation in a day." We all "pickle" in His presence and then go out and release the "pickling solution." We're simply us, in Him, and from there we go! The relationship we have with God is all about Him and us. But then as we catch the flavor and purpose of Jesus Christ, we go forth and share the good news with others, and it becomes about us, Him, and them. Sometimes intentionally, and other times by mistake, we just leak as we go, and people say, "Where have you been? You're different," and they end up coming to know our Jesus as their Lord and Savior. It's perfectly simple and simply perfect!

God highlighted the truth of this to me one day through an

abundant supply of bread. His Word (Jesus Christ) *is* our daily bread, and He will give us more than enough to consume for ourselves. He'll also provide for our family with enough excess to freely give. As you will see, if we hoard Him to ourselves, what we have will spoil. We must consume daily and be in the place of outward flow, for that's where the multiplication is. But that's also where our refreshing comes. When we spend time with God, we can give from the overflow. There's always a generosity of God in our lives. This awareness is what allows us to flow abundantly with His love, with His goodness, for there's always more than enough in Him.

GOD IS GOOD STORY: THE GENEROSITY OF GOD IN OUR LIVES

I was heading home when I remembered I needed to purchase bread. As I drove, I asked to see God's favor. Yep, I prayed the good ole *Please give me a good parking space, Lord. One right outside the bread store.*

I laughed out loud in surprise when I got one. It was the same store where I'd stopped and prayed for the owner and her daughter's family. Crazy miracles had flowed from the first time, when she cried as she recommitted her life to Jesus. *She* became a beautiful kiss from God every time I bought bread.

I popped into her store, bought the bread, and headed home. Then as I pulled up to my house, I saw that someone had left something at my door. Getting closer, I saw a bunch of red roses with a bag containing a loaf of bread, six small bread rolls, and some sweet scones. Now, people from the USA, these are not what *you* call scones. These are beautiful, light, fluffy, savory treats we put jam and cream on and eat with coffee or tea. People from the UK will understand what I'm talking about.

I gathered the goodies and headed inside to spend some time with God, just Him and me. I unpacked some of the bag, popped the roses in water, and sent a thank-you message to the friend who had sent the gift. As it turned out the gift giver was the store owner's daughter, for she had become a dear friend too. I then got on with my date with God.

As my time with Him ended, I rose and emptied the bag of bread. As I did, I had a bit of a giggle. There at the bottom of the bag were some CDs I'd missed. One was titled *Never Alone*, and the other *Walk with Us*.

God was showing me His love through that of another. In His way, God was saying to me, *As long as you come to Me, making sure you're well fed* [my loaf of bread that I bought, the price of which was my attention and my time], *I will multiply what you have, and in this way there will always more than enough for you and others* [the gift loaf of bread]. He continued. *I will also sweeten what you have* [the sweet scones] *and I will change it so that it is just what others need* [the small rolls that were just right for kids, for those young ones in the Lord I was leading]. *Oh, and by the way, I love you* [the red roses].

The CDs spoke to me of never being alone (the *Never Alone* CD), that regardless of how I might feel, God was always by my side. I was being invited to walk with the Trinity (Father, Son, and Holy Spirit—the *Walk with Us* CD). He was also calling me to walk with the bride of Christ. It was an invitation into family, fellowship, and a journey with Him and others too. I felt loved, encouraged, grateful, and filled.

I picked up the extra loaf of bread, set off for school pickups, and gave the loaf of bread away. It surprised the teacher I gave it to, but I knew I needed to give away what I'd received. I knew I needed to flow out of my abundance and give into my immediate community. There was more than enough for my family at home.

Now, please hear the double meaning in what I share. The following day the little rolls *fed* little ones—my children and a friend's children. And together we all enjoyed the sweetness of the sweet scones. I had bread for "the children" of God to share with my own and others.

It all needed to be shared or consumed. It was simply too much to hoard, and if we had, it would have gone hard and moldy. Similarly, if I hoard what God gives me, *I* become hard and moldy. If I hadn't given the bread away, allowing it to flow outward, what I'd been blessed with would have been wasted. There had to be an outward flow.

As we spend time with God, we'll always come out with more than enough for ourselves and for those we meet. There will always be enough because of the generosity of God. As we've explored, time spent with Him is never wasted. Rather, it accelerates us into His purposes while simultaneously ensuring we have what we need to continue. His presence in our lives provides the substance that transforms us into *who* we truly are while simultaneously empowering us to help transform the lives of those around us.

Naturally, we spend time with God simply because He adores us. And as we do, we fall deeply in love. In the saturating time we spend with Him, we discover how much He loves us, how we are His happy place. From there, our awareness of the overflow grows. There's always a constant supply of Him, but our awareness of that supply deepens and grows, and so our abandonment to giving Him away grows too.

In practicing His presence, in soaking in the Lord, be sure not to remain there only no matter how tempting it might be. Rather, pass it back to those around you, for what you give away will multiply. As you flow, so you will grow. We must drip as we go into the world, but to do so, we must first inhabit the secret place with Jesus. There we are fully immersed, baptized, in Him. We pickle in His presence, and in doing so we become pickled in His purpose. We're all called to spend time with Him, and from that place we flow forth into all the world, being fully ourselves, filled to overflowing with Him, impacting people and places for His name's sake. For we are all called to be about the Father's business.

Changed in His presence and chosen for His purpose, you, too, will drip everywhere you go. Like a pickled onion or a dripping sponge, you'll affect the world with His presence. Completely submerged in Him, you are a sunken treasure, Him in you, and you in Him. In that place, as you soak and then go, you'll know beyond a doubt that you are His happy place.

QUESTIONS FOR CONTEMPLATION

1. With a deeper understanding of the word *baptism*, think about times when you know you were baptizo (submerged, saturated, sunken) in the Holy Spirit. What was it like, and what changed for you? Journal about some of the times the Holy Spirit brings to your remembrance. Explore with Him the changes that occurred in you and through you from that time on and journal your insights as well.
2. What purpose do you believe God has for you? Talk to Him about it and journal your impressions and thoughts. Where can you flow immediately into your community and give what you carry away from your time with God?
3. What gifts do you believe you have? What gifts would you like to have? Who can you offer those to? Ask God to identify with whom or where you can serve with your gifts. Give what you carry away and see how it multiplies, bringing increase to yourself and to those around you. Be sure to journal what you discover.

RESPONSE TO THE REVELATION

- **Action Step 1:** This week set aside half to one hour to soak with God. You can put on music or remain in silence, but be sure to block the time out in your calendar so it's just you and Him. At the end of your time, journal what happens and what He says or shows you.
- **Action Step 2:** At the end of this soaking or soon thereafter, ask a family member or trusted friend if they can help you with an experiment. Ask if you can place your hand on their forearm. With their permission, do so as you remain aware of God's presence. Imagine you are the saturated sponge and "leak" God's anointing upon them. You don't need to pray; just be aware of God and in your heart ask Him to

flow through you upon the other. Ask your friend or family member what they feel if anything. Journal what you discover.

LET'S PRAY

Father, thank You for the baptism in the Holy Spirit. Thank You that I am fully submerged and constantly saturated in You. Help me become more aware of this reality, and by spending time with You, naturally drip with Your presence everywhere I go. Thank you that as I change in Your presence, I'll more fully recognize that I've been chosen for Your purpose before time. Thoroughly submerge me into the love of Jesus like a sunken treasure, and let me drip with Your goodness everywhere I go. In the mighty name of Jesus I pray, amen.

9

BEING THE FRAGRANCE OF CHRIST

Thanks be to God, who always leads us as captives in Christ's triumphal procession and uses us to spread the aroma of the knowledge of him everywhere. For we are to God the pleasing aroma of Christ among those who are being saved and those who are perishing.
2 Corinthians 2:14–15

A FAVORITE MEMORY of mine is when, over a cuppa together, my father described how he discovered his favorite rose. He and my mother were wandering through a garden center looking at rose varieties for their garden when an intense fragrance caused him to stop in his tracks. After some sleuthing, he discovered the rose responsible. It was Double Delight, cultivated for its beauty and exquisite perfume. I don't believe I've ever seen him so animated as he told me about this discovery and subsequent purchase.

"You must smell it for yourself, Bethie," he said. "You would love this rose."

My mother affirmed his story. "I've never seen your father so intent on finding a rose. Its fragrance totally captivated him."

On the back of his excitement, I went to the garden center and found the rose for myself. He was right! This rose *was* a double delight of fragrance and beauty. Its fragrance lingered, suspended in the air. It permeated the surrounding space and drew unsuspecting customers into its fragrant orbit. Delighting all, apprehending rose aficionado and novice alike, I'm sure many purchases were made. Suffice to say, I, too, bought the rose, and to this day the fragrance reminds me of my father and I smile whenever I draw near.

Our baptism in Christ leaves us saturated in a fragrance. As we spend time beholding the One who is Love, we're imbued with the fragrance of Jesus Christ. It permeates us without our knowing. Understanding we are the Father's delight, we carry His Son's fragrance with us into the world where others will discern Him too. People around us start to experience the love of God and learn that He adores them, He sees them, and they have His attention as well. Through the fragrance of love, we draw them to Jesus. Remember always that it was for love that He took on all our shortcomings, so that through His death and resurrection we would come out "smelling of roses." We say yes and are immersed in Him, and so we take on the fragrance of Christ.

Always in Jesus, and Him always in us, the fragrance remains, lingering in the air we inhabit. Like those people who offer samples of perfume at shopping centers, we offer encounters as we go. We diffuse His fragrance through community and culture, unintentionally drawing others to experience Him. It's not forced, and there is no striving. We're simply an embodiment of the invitation to discover the source wherever we go. We take what we've experienced of Him and allow it to flow. Some of those who experience Him will choose to lean in for a deeper experience, others will come to explore Him for themselves, while still others will take Him home for themselves and are in turn imbued and release His fragrance where *they* go.

How do we do this? By simply being with Jesus and spending time with Him, we become the fragrance of Christ. This intentional time causes us to become more aware of what we truly carry, and many will even seek us out to learn what we are. Such was the impact of my spending time with Him, and so, too, will be the impact of yours. And yet we must always remember that at no stage does Jesus want you to lose *you*. Rather, He wants you to spread His fragrance to others in the "you shaped you" that you are. You are a double delight to Him! As you are irreplaceable, He bought you for a price, and forever more you remain His happy place.

INTIMACY CREATES OFFSPRING

Learning to abide in what many would call "the secret place with God" is intoxicating, and it becomes tempting to stay there exclusively. You'll want to shout loudly to anyone who will listen, "I have entered the Holy of Holies! I now hold the key! This is what we're all designed for! Come with me and see!" And I would agree. The secret chambers of His fragrant love *is* what we're all designed for. But to dwell there exclusively is to lose sight of why we're here. To dwell in the heart of the loving Father is where we must learn to live from, and yet life in the world is to be lived as well.

Naturally, in spending time with God, we'll come out carrying His fragrance. Like hugging someone who's wearing a strong cologne or perfume, we carry God's fragrance with us as we go. And that's as it should be. Like the smell of freshly baked bread, freshly brewed coffee, and freshly cut grass, there's something about us people will notice as we interact with them. The fragrance of heaven will affect them whether or not we wear our "Jesus" T-shirt. Often they can't place why, but they'll simply enjoy being near us. Like the ballet mom who wanted to stand close to me for what I carried, the fragrance of heaven will trigger a yearning deep within all who come near.

GOD IS GOOD STORY: HEALING AND ROSES FROM A LOVING GOD

I've mentioned how in the early years of her education, my daughter changed schools. Through this change, I had hoped to fly under the radar, just for a while. I wanted to remain somewhat in my God closet so I could establish who I was before I became known as "the God lady"—the one who prayed for anything that moved. God had been very active at Rebekah's kindergarten and her first school, and I was hoping for a break from stepping out. We *are* all called to pour Him out everywhere we go, but I simply wanted space to breathe. In my daughter's first school, I'd rattled cages and caused a stir around me. In this new school I hoped to keep the attention at bay, at least for a while, until I found my feet.

It was simply not to be. Healing, loving, encouraging, giving—we are fragrance to a hurting world. God wants us to release Him as we move throughout society.

The week Rebekah started, I bought her teacher, whom I'll call Mrs. R, some flowers to recognize her on International Teacher's Day. But it was also a gift to thank her for taking extra care of my girl. She had gone well beyond the call of duty, and I was grateful. The flowers were pink roses, the color chosen by my four-year-old son. "They must be dark pink, because she's beautiful!" Matthew declared earnestly. I readily agreed.

On this occasion, I missed her, so the school receptionist put the flowers in a vase and left them on her desk in the hope they would last the weekend. They did.

Two weeks later, Mrs. R kept "popping up" in my mind, so I prayed for her. I sensed she hadn't been well, and as I prayed, I felt God prompt me to purchase more flowers. This time, I "saw" a picture of red roses in my mind's eye. I argued with God about buying more flowers, wondering if it was just my imagination. However, the inclination never let up. I knew it was something God wanted me to do, so I did, feeling a bit silly since I'd bought her flowers only two weeks prior. I desperately didn't want to come across as what we call in Australia "a try hard," but with God on my case, I knew to obey.

Interestingly, I also knew these roses had to be red. They were a gift from God, a gift to say *I love you*, and what better way to say that than red roses.

Running late for school pickup on a scorching hot day, I raced to the store to purchase the roses. It wasn't a day to be doing this with a four-year-old. I was a little miffed at the assignment. *You better make it possible for me to get to the school on time*, I told God.

Well, I didn't get there on time. I ran late. Sweltering in the heat, I ran into the classroom, and there was no Mrs. R! I ran to the front office and spoke to the woman there. Still no Mrs. R! In fact, she'd gone home early, ill. I lifted the flowers to show the receptionist, who just smiled and said, "Oh no, not again!"

I smiled back, feeling foolish, and left the flowers on the desk. As I rapidly retreated, I explained I was a Christian and had felt Mrs. R was still not right. "I've been praying for her throughout the day, and I felt I needed to give her these roses to encourage her in a tough time."

"I'll email her immediately and let her know about the roses," the receptionist replied. "She'll be thrilled, but she won't be in tomorrow."

Now I felt embarrassed—and a tad irritated with God. He knew she wasn't there, yet He still wanted me to drop off those roses. *Perhaps I got the timing wrong*, I thought. *Or perhaps I got it wrong altogether and didn't hear from God at all.* Perhaps . . . perhaps . . . perhaps!

I mulled over the situation, feeling more foolish by the minute, until I suddenly said to God, *Well, I knew You wanted me to do this, so regardless, I tried to be obedient.* I encouraged myself, as I still do in these circumstances. I figure as long as I leave people feeling loved, it really doesn't matter what others think of me. In the moment, I also tried to convince myself it didn't matter that I was being fast-tracked to being dubbed "the crazy Christian woman who keeps giving the teacher flowers when she's never there to receive them."

On leaving the school, I kept praying for Mrs. R. Then the following day I received an email:

> I just wanted to express my thanks for the beautiful roses; you are extremely thoughtful! Hopefully, a few days of rest will have me feeling back to my usual healthy self. Have a lovely weekend, and thanks again!
>
> Kind regards . . .

I responded by writing:

> You are welcome—in fact it was on a "gut feel" that you were having a pretty tough time, and as a Christian family we like to

encourage people when they are having such times, especially when placed on our hearts to pray for them as you have been for me (this reads awkwardly and I had hoped to explain verbally).... I have been praying for you as prompted, and felt that God wanted to give you the flowers and little chocolate ... a "kiss from God" so to speak to encourage you in whatever you are dealing with ... but, as I said, much easier to verbally explain than in writing. I have learnt through experience that when I feel a prompting like I did yesterday, it is best to act on them. I'd rather look like a dag [author's note: *dag* is an Australian term meaning "look silly"] than miss it ... Rest well, and have a lovely weekend.

I emailed thinking, *I'll explain better when I see her next. Either way, I've shown my colors!*

The following Monday, I arrived a little early for school pickup with a really tight turnaround because of ballet and tennis drop-offs for my two children. Upon seeing me, Mrs. R came outside to say thank you again. I confirmed I was a Christian and said, "The first lot of flowers were from me to say thank you, but the second lot were from God to say *I love you*."

I explained I'd been praying for her and had sensed she'd been ill. I told her I'd also been praying for her when I felt God tell me to get the flowers (and a silver heart chocolate to go with them). It was to let her know she was "on His mind" and that "He loved her!"

She looked at me in shock and said, "Was it instinct?"

"No, it's called being prophetic. It's hearing from God. We can all do it," I replied.

The Holy Spirit swirled as I spoke. Mrs. R could feel it, too, and she teared up. "Amazing," she said. A colleague had dropped the roses off for her that same night. "It was so strange, because the illness lifted that afternoon."

She briefly shared how, from that time, she was fine. It wasn't long before she put two and two together and realized the timing of the prayer and the roses. She knew it was a miracle. She stared at me, incredulous.

"Stay there," she said. "I want to talk to you some more." Then she turned to dismiss the children from class.

By this stage I knew I was running late, but I also knew this was a God appointment, and so I put my agenda on hold and waited.

Mrs. R came back and said, "I want to know more."

So I told her how I'd felt the need to pray for her that afternoon and had bought the flowers for her, but then I'd missed her and felt silly. "The flowers were from God," I confirmed. "It's His way of letting you know He loves you and that He had *you* on His heart." I then confirmed we could all hear from God.

Mrs. R was teary and said repeatedly, "That someone would bother . . . that someone would bother . . ." She confirmed she *had* felt loved and cared for. She felt "so touched that someone would bother."

Unfortunately, at that moment, a child threw a tantrum, and Mrs. R became flustered. Even though she came back to me, the "God moment" was gone for her. Regardless, I knew it was a moment she would never forget.

What I didn't share with her at the time was that I had the strongest feeling she was in danger of miscarrying. I just knew that I knew this. So as I prayed, I'd prayed earnestly, with a purpose and intent. She later shared with me how she *had* started to miscarry, that it would have been her second such loss. It amazed her how the bleeding stopped the same afternoon. She had worked it out, but at the time she couldn't share because she was not yet twelve weeks through her pregnancy. I also didn't share what I knew, respecting her boundary of privacy.

Months later, Mrs. R gave birth to a beautiful little girl she named Philippa Beth. Interestingly, Philippa was the name I was going to be given at birth, but my parents changed their mind and called me Beth instead.

This story was the first of many such occurrences throughout the school. Mrs. R became convinced we'd changed schools for her and her baby. She once dared speculate what might have happened had we not come. Without a doubt she believes she would have lost her baby girl. For her, I carried the fragrance of healing and the roses of love from a loving God. For we are the aroma of He who brings life if we will flow as Christ directs.

WE ARE ALABASTER JARS OF JESUS' FRAGRANCE OF LIFE

Think of the woman, Mary, who broke forth an alabaster jar of perfume, so fragrant and extreme that we still speak of her today. Her gratitude was so great that she had to express her love to Jesus in an act of reckless abundance: "While he was in Bethany, reclining at the table in the home of Simon the Leper, a woman came with an alabaster jar of very expensive perfume, made of pure nard. She broke the jar and poured the perfume on his head" (Mark 14:3).

This fragrance, the fragrance of her love for Jesus, would have filled the room in which those who could not or would not recognize Jesus for who He was sat. Alabaster is a soft stone, easy to carve. Used as lampshades and window panes in years gone by, it allows light to shine through when made fine enough. We are called to carry the light and shine.

When carved into a box or a bottle, alabaster is easy to break open to allow its contents to pour forth. Bottles or jars created to contain such oils would have long fine necks so that it would be easy to break them open to release the oil within. An alabaster jar contained the fragrant anointing oil fit to anoint King Jesus for death—a death that brought life. Will we be an alabaster jar of the Lord and allow His fragrance to permeate the rooms we enter? Will we allow ourselves to be filled, saturated, baptized with His presence so that we overflow with the fragrance of heaven?

The fragrance of Jesus' death is one that brings us life, and as we allow Him to shine and flow to those around us, we bring the fragrance of life too. Such was what happened to Mrs. R's unborn child, Philippa Beth.

If you'll allow God to soak you through as you spend time with Him, you'll become imbued with His fragrance. His fragrance is so pure, so profound, that you will affect those you come into contact with without even trying. In being baptized, His essence saturates, imbuing you with His love in such a way you will leave His fragrance everywhere you go.

HIS FRAGRANCE WILL FLOW

Word of Mrs. R's miracle spread quickly. God had many more prayer assignments, but one stands out to me as something of great beauty.

It wasn't long before God placed the junior school principal, whom I'll call Ms. M, on my heart. The first time I stepped out and offered to pray for her was intimidating, but in her generosity of spirit she quickly put me at ease. "I hear you've been loving on my staff," she said. "Thank you." And "Yes, you absolutely can pray for me" was her response to my request to pray for her the first time. The fragrance of God's love had gone forth, affecting both hearts and minds.

I can't recall if it was this first time or another time when I taught her about God spaces, but it was a powerful moment for us both. She mentioned seeking direction from tarot cards each morning. I gently suggested that now she could seek God's face instead. It was with a beautiful heart response that she agreed, and each day forth she sought God's guidance even before she'd fully committed her heart to Jesus.

Not long before this the principal had granted me an open-door policy. If I ever had a prophetic word or an inclination to pray for her or the school, I was welcome to walk straight into her office if the door was open. I could pray and/or prophesy as I felt led, such was the favor of God. Ms. M sensed the fragrance of God in my life and was hungry to learn more. Ever ready to receive His love, she said she could see a light shining from both my daughter and me. Each week in the school chapel service, she watched Rebekah shine more brightly than at any other times.

She said she'd watched my husband, Andrew, as well. She shared how she saw him look at me when I wasn't aware, watching me with love in his eyes. Our family was a witness of God's love. She was watching, and although we weren't perfect, she wanted more. Not long after that she saw the magnitude of Jesus in her life during an encounter and gave her heart to Jesus.

It's time she asked me into her heart, I heard the Holy Spirit say one day. I instantly shared what I heard with her.

"I think it is too," this beautiful woman replied.

We sat in her office as she gave her life to Jesus. From that time forth, she prayed for staff, students, and parents each day. She was diligent in seeking God for answers and engaged His help for every aspect of her life. The transformation was awe-inspiring. Importantly, the school chaplain, with whom I was meeting every two weeks to pray for the school at large, supported her transformation.

The remarkable thing was that in this transformation, her prophetic gift burst forth and flourished. I became the recipient of many prophetic encouragements, frequently leaving me speechless and in tears.

When we choose to engage our hearts, inclining our ear toward God's promptings throughout our day, we release the fragrance of heaven. This has an accumulative effect, which often creates favor for us to release kingdom concepts, ideas, and blueprints into a community. This is how we can affect the world regardless of our busy lives. It really is possible to have a positive impact on a community by imparting the fragrance of love wherever we go.

GOD IS GOOD STORY: THE FRAGRANCE OF LOVE

A few years later, my son started school a short drive away. I regularly drove past my daughter's school on my way home from dropping him off. As I did, I often prayed for the teachers, those in authority, the children, and the school community at large.

One such morning, I was praying as I drove when Ms. M. came to mind. As I drove closer, I suddenly felt the Father's heart—a feeling I call "His joy indescribable." With the feeling came a flashback to earlier that morning. I'd seen Ms. M. throw her arms wide with a great, joy-filled love as she leaned down to hug a small girl at the school gate.

With the flooding joy and flash of memory, I knew I needed to run into the school, give her a big hug, and tell her how loved she was. When I'd seen that hug on the street, I'd smiled. She was tangibly pouring out love, and I *knew* I had to do the same for her. Indeed, I'd felt the desire to run across the road and hug her earlier that morning. Perhaps I'd missed God's first prompt!

I pulled over in the autumn sunshine and ran into the school, past a staff member, calling out, "I'm here to give Ms. M a hug!" I ran straight to her office, and through the open door and on seeing my target, I declared, "I need to give you a hug!"

She stood straight up, stepped over her papers, and with arms open wide she let me hug her.

"You are so loved!" I said. "You're doing a great job! I saw you hugging the girls this morning, loving on them, and then God wanted me to give *you* a hug!"

Now, please note. Hugging is not my thing. Touch is not my love language. But when God tells me to hug, I hug. It's just taken time to know I need to obey this prompt regardless of my discomfort. I also understand that if I respond in faith, I will often benefit too. As God pours Himself through, over, and around me, I'm also saturated in the fragrance of His love.

And so I stood there and hugged. Honestly, this hug *was* amazing. I genuinely loved the principal. I actually felt safe around her, to be fully me. The joy and love I feel for her is not just heaven sent; it's genuinely me as well. So it was *God's* love and joy for her but mine as well. The hug was equally a blessing to me as it was to her!

With the hug finished, she stood back. "Oh, that was good. You're a good hugger. I felt that! Look, I'm covered in goose bumps!"

I smiled. Ms. M knew who the goosebumps were from.

"God just wants you to know how very loved you are," I told her. "He wants you to know that you're doing a great job." Then as I went to leave, I called out, "Have a great day!"

I walked past the staff member I'd seen on my sprint into the school. With an overwhelming desire to hug her as well, I offered.

"I'm always up for a hug," she responded, and she ran over and threw her arms around me. Mid-hug she said, "Oh, you *are* a good hugger!"

I gave her a kiss on the cheek as the principal called out, "It's a wonderful hug! I've got goose bumps all over me, up and down my legs."

I called out that I loved it too. Then I left, running into the sunshine, feeling God flowing all around and through me. It was "joy indescribable."

As I drove home, still basking in God's love, I realized I could smell both women's perfumes on my coat. I smiled, realizing I'd also left a deposit of perfume on them. It was the fragrance of love, and I knew that, like me, they would carry God's fragrance throughout their day. Their interaction with heaven would affect others *they* came into contact with, for His love is infectious. God imbued us all with His fragrance of love as we hugged each other well.

Like a person's perfume lingers on your clothes long after they've left, we can all leave the fragrance of love in our wake. Second Corinthians 2:14–15 says, "Thanks be to God who always leads us in triumph in Christ, and through us diffuses the fragrance of His knowledge in every place. For we are to God the fragrance of Christ among those who are being saved and among those who are perishing" (NKJV).

You are the fragrance of God as you go about life. Responding to His voice as you go, saturated in His presence and imbued with His purpose, you leave the fragrance of Christ in your wake. Abundance of life was the exchange won at the cross, and so His lasting, life-giving fragrance lingers in lives on which you have an effect on His behalf (John 10:10). You are called to emerge and diffuse His fragrance. More fully yourself than you were before, you understand that *you* are His happiest of places. This understanding will bring a quiet comfort and joy appealing to those around you, and they'll seek out why you seem a little different. Permeated with His presence, if you will diffuse His love like a fragrant offering, pouring Him out to those around you, His fragrance *will change lives.*

You are an alabaster jar, filled to the brim and then some. In Jesus, filled with Jesus; in God, filled with God; and in the Holy Spirit, filled with the Holy Spirit, you become the fragrance of Christ. You can never run dry since a constant flow of fragrant goodness is always available. God's goodness, His love, leaves a fragrance in your life and in the lives of those around you. Your fragrance is the invitation, the first hint of how He adores, accepts, loves, and cares for those you encounter. Fully yourself, imbued with His substance, you can choose to go forth and be a fragrant love offering from a beautiful Father. If you will allow Him to flow through you with intentionality, you'll see His goodness. But even if you don't, just being you *will* affect the world around you. Simply put, the fragrance of His love is uncontainable, unquenchable, and will permeate all you do. You are and always will be His happy place, and as He resides within, you are the fragrance of Christ.

QUESTIONS TO CONTEMPLATE

1. When have you been aware of someone walking into a room and shifting the atmosphere? What was the shift from and to? We use the term "it smelled off" or "it smells fishy" to describe a bad deal. In the same way, think about the fragrance they carried in their spirit. What was it? Did it permeate the atmosphere with goodness? Now, thinking of the Double Delight rose my father adored, when have you become aware of the fragrance of Jesus Christ infusing the environment with the fragrance of heaven?
2. When have you been aware that the fragrance of Jesus Christ within you and upon you has changed an atmosphere? For example, when my children were babies, a pre-believing mother told me she swore much less when I was around. I had no awareness of this until she mentioned it to me. Has something similar happened to you? If not, ask God to show you when the fragrance of Jesus Christ in your life made a difference. Then journal about what He shows you.

3. When have you stepped out to make a difference in someone's life on the prompting of the Holy Spirit? What has been the effect of your interaction with that person? How has that changed them, drawn them closer to God? Have they then carried the fragrance you released into their lives and shared it with others? Journal your thoughts and insights.

RESPONSE TO THE REVELATION

- **Action Step 1**: Spend some time with God and ask the Holy Spirit to identify a fragrance you carry as you go. Think of the fruit of the Spirit in Galatians 5:22–23. You might carry a fragrance of joy, hope, love, peace, or faith. Alternatively, you might release a fragrance of excellence, worship, or contemplation. Being aware of your heavenly fragrance will assist you in being intentional in releasing it everywhere you go. Of course, we carry it all, because the fullness of Jesus Christ is within us, but you'll have your unique mixture of fragrances that you alone carry—much like a spiritual thumbprint or DNA.
- **Action Step 2:** Each day this week, remind yourself of the fragrance you carry as revealed by the Holy Spirit. Ask God if there's someone with whom you can leave the fragrance of His love. This could be through a word of encouragement, an ARK (Act of Random Kindness) or simply a smile. If you feel bold, ask God for someone to overtly minister to. Notice their reaction and any shift in atmospheres and see if it's in accord with your fragrance as revealed by your time with the Holy Spirit.

LET'S PRAY

Father, thank You for the privilege of being the aroma of Jesus Christ everywhere I go. Thank You that You break me open like an alabaster jar to receive more of Your love so I might then release Your fragrant love wherever I may be. I say yes to being carved into Your vessel, to carry Your fragrant perfume. I say yes to being filled, saturated, baptized with Your presence so I might overflow with the fragrance of heaven. Pour Yourself out through me as a love offering to all those who come near. In Jesus' mighty name I pray, amen.

10

GOD CALLS ME BY NAME

"I tell you that you are Peter, and on this rock I will build my church, and the gates of Hades will not overcome it."
Matthew 16:18

GOD HAS INTENTIONALLY PLACED you at this very moment of time. He sees you, He adores you, and He calls you by name. You are His happy place, and He delights as you discover your true nature and personal calling. He will give you a name that reveals your purpose and identity.

Let's look briefly at how Jesus did that for Simon Peter. Jesus said, "And I tell you that you are Peter [meaning rock], and on this rock I will build my church" (Matthew 16:18). In this moment, Jesus called Peter according to who *He* saw Peter to be. With Peter's new name came his true purpose—to be a foundational rock for God's kingdom.

In the same way, God wants you to hear the names He has for you. Contained within each are keys to who He calls you to be. They will speak of your personal identity, destiny, and purpose. Sometimes God will send someone to speak prophetically to us, highlighting how He sees us and giving us a name maybe different from the one a parent gave us at birth. We can also discover the names He has for us in the time we spend with Him in quiet solitude, for it's in the quiet intimate times that our truest identity is revealed.

But it's not only the names He gives through prophecy or in the secret place that will carry prophetic weight. Your birth name, your married name, even your nicknames contain keys to your identity and destiny in Him. Just like Peter, you're here to fulfill a magnificent kingdom purpose, and the name God gives you will prophetically point to your kingdom call.

The very best place to unpack the names God has given you is in the place of yada with Him. *Yada* is a Hebrew word meaning to know intimately. When we spend time in yada with God, we come to know our true selves, our core identity, from which all else should flow. As we gaze on the Father's face, He reflects to us aspects of Himself that He's placed deep within our beings. In this place, He calls us by name, and He gives us our names. We each carry a unique expression of Him, and since God's diversity is endless, so, too, is the diversity of every one of us. Each of us is equally breathtaking and, with never-ending creativity, He creates us all, weaving into our DNA aspects of Himself that will reflect into the earth for His glory. We therefore also each have a unique name and a unique destiny that no one else can fulfill.

It is here, from the place of truest kingdom identity, found in the "yada" with God, that we discover our kingdom names, and in doing so, we discover our truest kingdom purpose. From this identity, we can then stand together and radiate the whole of an ever-expanding God. Remembering that "his intent was that now, through the church [us], the manifold [multicolored, diverse] wisdom of God should be made known to the rulers and authorities in the heavenly realms, according to his eternal purpose that he accomplished in Christ Jesus our Lord" (Ephesians 3:10–11).

TO "YADA"—OR TO EXPERIENTIALLY KNOW GOD INTIMATELY

The idea of knowing God is reflected throughout Scripture. Again, the Hebrew verb *yada* is translated into the English word *know*.[1] Used nearly one thousand times, it encapsulates far more than what the

English word *know* suggests. The meaning behind the Hebraic word inherently includes an experiential knowing. We are "knowing" He is God. We are becoming "intimately acquainted" with Him. It is a knowing beyond mere intellectual assent or understanding. God desires us to experience Him at the deepest levels of our knowing ability.

As Psalm 46:10 aptly puts it, He desires us to "be still, and know" —experientially and ongoing—that He is God. This yada is a knowing that includes experiencing God's character and nature for ourselves. We no longer learn about God but have an interpersonal relationship with Him and learn about Him for ourselves through experiencing Him personally. In turn, as we grow to know God, we learn more about ourselves, and we begin to see others as He sees them. We first learn *whose* we are—His—and from that place of security we come to know *who* we are in Him. Once begun, the journey of knowing Him unravels the mystery of self, as it also reveals the identity of those around us. He shows us others in such a way that we cannot help but fall in love with all of His creation.

An interesting depth can come from really catching the concept of *knowing* God. To know God is the same "knowing" Adam had with Eve that begat a child. It is "to know intimately" in such a way that there is offspring. Time spent with God will produce fruit in our lives. Just as a fruit tree planted into good soil, watered, and given sunlight and nutrients will naturally bear fruit. We all, planted into the soil of God's heart, don't need to force fruit. Fruit simply happens from this time of *knowing that He is God.*

As a verb, *yada* is a doing word. We are knowing He is God in an ongoing manner. Much as we become saturated in Him as we are baptized in Him in an ongoing manner, so, too, we are knowing Him with an everlasting knowing. We become more and more intimately acquainted with Him, like a lover or a close friend. It's an ongoing knowing . . . and knowing . . . and knowing. As we come to know God intimately, we learn more about Him—much in the same way I knew my husband when I married him, but now I know him in a greater sense. After thirty-plus years of marriage, I'm certainly more acquainted with my husband. I know and appreciate his likes and dislikes. I can sense his nuanced reactions.

Similarly, we become more familiar with God's likes and dislikes. We learn to recognize His voice and His ways, and we discover for ourselves what He cares about most. As we grow more familiar with who He is, we can recognize when He speaks and when what we hear doesn't sound like Him. By spending time with the real, we learn to recognize the false when it tries to masquerade as the authentic.

In *this* place, we learn why He loves us, and even more importantly, why He likes us. It's through learning why He likes us and how He created us that we discover our true identity. Not just that we're His beloved, His child, His friend, or His servant. We're not simply someone He's obliged to love. He actually likes us too. According to Ephesians 2:10, you, me, all of us are His handiwork (in some Bible translations, his "masterpieces"). We really are His happy place! You—yes, you—are God's happy thought, and it's His delight to love us all into ourselves. Through the lens of His love, we discover what our unique kingdom identity looks like, and in doing so we discover *why* we are His happy place.

Of course, to understand who we are requires our cooperation. For the exchange to occur, of knowing Him to know ourselves, we must come to Him and spend time with Him. To do so implies an acknowledgment that He exists, for "anyone who comes to [God] must believe that he exists" (Hebrews 11:6). But even believing God exists is nothing special since "even the demons believe that—and shudder" (James 2:19). Rather, it's through our recognition of *who* Jesus is that we come into a greater revelation of who we are. Our belief about who Jesus is to us matters. From that place, we can then choose to spend time getting to know Him. So saying you believe God exists is just the start. And while your identity is still contained within the seed of potential, it's only when we determine who Jesus is for ourselves that the fullness of our kingdom identity truly begins to unfold. (If you wish to accept Jesus Christ into your heart to receive the fullness of your kingdom inheritance, please head to the "Do You Know Jesus?" section at the back of this book.)

WHO DO WE SAY JESUS IS?

We see this play out in the life of Peter:

> When Jesus came to the region of Caesarea Philippi, he asked his disciples, "Who do people say the Son of Man is?" [The disciples] replied, "Some say John the Baptist; others say Elijah; and still others, Jeremiah or one of the prophets." "But what about you?" he asked. "Who do you say I am?" Simon Peter answered, "You are the Messiah, the Son of the living God." (Matthew 16:13–16)

In this passage Peter declares Jesus is the Messiah. He has just caught the revelatory truth of who Jesus is. Jesus clarifies that this revelation came from God by saying, "Blessed are you, Simon son of Jonah, for this was not revealed to you by flesh and blood, but by my Father in heaven" (16:17).

Immediately upon hearing Peter's recognition of who He is, Jesus then releases greater insight into who Peter is and shares with Peter how heaven really sees him: "And I tell you that you are Peter, and on this rock I will build my church, and the gates of Hades will not overcome it. I will give you the keys of the kingdom of heaven; whatever you bind on earth will be bound in heaven, and whatever you loose on earth will be loosed in heaven" (16:18–19).

Once we catch sight of who Jesus is and choose to believe in our hearts and declare with our mouths that He is Lord (Romans 10:9), Jesus will draw us into a conversation about who *we* are to Him. He will reveal deeper meaning in the names we were given by our parents. He will even explore married names and nicknames, and like Peter He will give us new names too. All names reveal our purpose and destiny. Indeed, He draws us into these conversations long before we even acknowledge who He is, for it delights the Father's heart to see His precious children step into the fullness for which they are designed, whether or not they recognize Him as Father. But I suggest the *fullness* of our understanding of our names becomes available only to those who call upon the name of Jesus as Lord.

WiITH A NEW NAME, A NEW IDENTITY

Let's consider Jesus' response in Matthew 16:18. What you might have noticed is that Peter receives a new name. Jesus responds by immediately changing his name, Simon, Son of Jonah, to Peter. He bestows upon him not just a new name, but a new identity, a new purpose, and greater authority. In understanding who Jesus was, Peter shifted more fully into his kingdom destiny, and Jesus could reveal to Peter who he was. From that vantage point, Peter could then glean a deeper understanding of who he was and where his destiny lay.

It's also interesting that in the very next scene, Jesus shifts gears and starts to share deeper things with the disciples. Through Peter's revelation of who Jesus is, *all* the disciples appear to step into a deeper relationship with Jesus. It is as if Peter's revelation and public declaration opens a door to a corporate upgrade for all the disciples, and they step into a friendship with Jesus: "From that time on Jesus began to explain to His disciples that he must go to Jerusalem and suffer many things at the hands of the elders, the chief priests and the teachers of the law, and that he must be killed and on the third day be raised to life" (Matthew 16:21–25).

It's as if Jesus has said, "Now that you've all seen Me as I am, let Me show you who *you* are to Me and the deeper purposes my Father and I are up to." Jesus allows them to see what's coming. He's speaking to them as "friends." As He explains in John 15:15, friends let each other in on what's next: "I no longer call you servants, because a servant does not know his master's business. Instead, I have called you friends, for everything that I learned from my Father I have made known to you."

A servant is obedient to a master and will obey without understanding. Friends share deeper understanding, call each other higher, and do so from an appreciation of who each is called to be. With the recognition of who Jesus is comes a shift in relationship with all the disciples.

Jesus shares the deeper things, but He also shares the higher calling of each one. We see this transaction clearly in the moment He renames Simon as "Peter," the "rock."

NAMES CONTAIN YOUR PROPHETIC PROMISE—WHO DOES JESUS SAY YOU ARE?

It's important to understand that within Hebraic culture, names held more meaning than just identifiers or labels. Names contained prophetic promises of who a person was called to be and/or what an area was created for. Think of Abram ("exalted father") who becomes Abraham ("exalted father of a multitude"). His wife, Sarai, meaning "princess," becomes Sarah, "noble one."[2] Even place names have significance and receive upgrades according to purpose and historical significance. Jacob renames Luz, El Bethel, meaning "house of God," after he encounters angelic activity there. A shift of names, or the gift of a new name, becomes an entry point to identity, and with that identity comes purpose, meaning, and destiny.

As God gives us a deeper understanding of who we are through the names He provides us, we can feel His loving attention. With the joyful gaze of a parent, He gently nurtures us into the fullness of our potential. Calling each of us by name, with a delight in His gaze, He cups us in the palms of His hands to remind us how He sees us—always first and foremost a beloved child with purpose to step into. Feeling His gaze, we know with a depth that we are His happy place as He sings over us the things yet to come. With patience He renames us and corrects our paths, reminding us what our names truly mean.

Even in Peter's betrayal we witness God's patience. Through Jesus' loving-kindness, Peter is restored, calling him back to his true self—the rock on which the church would be built. Jesus reminds Peter of his call, reasserting who Peter is in his Father's gaze. To know the Father's heart is to know our true name as He nurtures each of us back to our original design and purpose.

We can see how Simon Peter steps into his call after he receives his new name, and although he might struggle in the transition, devastatingly denying Jesus three times, once restored he gets there in the end. This only serves to encourage us. We don't need to be perfect to step into our new identity. We all grow by increments, and as our understanding of who Jesus is grows, so, too, will our understanding of ourselves.

The name Simon means "listen" or "hearing." He's been listening and hearing Jesus throughout their three years together. But then he receives his new name, Peter, meaning "stone or rock." It's upon this foundation (a foundation of stone, a solid foundation) that Jesus will build His church. Jesus is using a metaphor. But while understanding that Jesus is the "cornerstone" and the true foundation made of stone,[3] Simon does become foundational in establishing the early church. So Simon is no longer the one who merely listens, but Peter—one upon whom Jesus can build, a foundation on whom the church will grow.

In this passage as well we see a mention that Peter also becomes one who holds keys—he will be a gatekeeper in the age soon to come. Jesus is making an obvious reference to the mention of keys in Isaiah 22:22: "I will place on his shoulder the key to the house of David; what he opens no one can shut, and what he shuts no one can open." In other words, he's saying "The authority I have come with as the representative of the house of David, the house from which the Messiah comes, I give to you to lose and bind." Peter grows in both, becoming the solid foundation through whom revelation will flow.

Think of Peter's role in revealing what was happening within the chaos at Pentecost as he declares, "These people are not drunk . . . [but] this is what was spoken by the prophet Joel. . . . I will pour out my Spirit on all people" (Acts 2:15–17). He also has the honor of opening the gospel to the gentiles through his understanding of his vision upon the roof of Simon the Tanner (Acts 10). In addition, he functions in the authority as shown by Jesus to extend the kingdom of heaven. He loosens heavenly realities and binds demonic powers as he goes.

In the moment Peter recognizes who Jesus is, he steps "through" Jesus, the revelatory door of understanding, into his new identity and purpose. And with this moment of recognition, Jesus provides a new name. Inextricably intertwined in his new name are purpose, destiny, and authority—all available to him and within his grasp.

The power in our name is profound, and within it encompasses deep meaning. It's in our time with Jesus, in our yada time with God, that we discover who we are. If we will explore what He's saying to us, He will reveal aspects of ourselves He's hidden for us to find and step into. Remember this from chapter 1 of this book: He is the God who sees, the God who hears, and the God who knows. He calls us by name, and He delights in us, for we are His happy place.

GOD IS GOOD STORY: NAMES IN THE SECRET PLACE—MY BETH

On my journey with God, I discovered He had a way He would refer to me. I would hear Him in my heart telling me sweet nothings and affirming how pleased He was with me as I stretched and grew. When I stepped out for the one, He would often whisper to me, *Well done, My Beth*. As I journaled with Him, He would call me My Beth. When I stepped into exuberant worship, or broke things open as a prophetic intercessor, He would whisper encouragingly, *My Beth, My Beth, I'm so proud of you, My Beth*.

I thought nothing of it for a very long time. It was simply a sweet way He spoke to me. I felt He was letting me know He saw and loved me. However, one day after journaling with Him for some time, I became inquisitive. Why was He calling me My Beth even as I journaled? Why did He insist on calling me *My* Beth, and why did He insist I write My Beth with a capital *M* in that quiet time? I'm sure He sparked the idea to go deeper, and in going deeper, not only did I discover who I was and how I was known but healing flowed through my soul.

When I wrote My Beth, it was always with a capital *M* for *My*. I knew I was *His* Beth, but I became progressively more interested in what He was trying to tell me in speaking this way. There was nearly an insistence in His manner. So I stopped what I was doing and looked up the meaning of my name.

Now, you must know I never really liked my name. As an Aussie girl growing up in the 1970s, there were no Beths around me. There was the sickly Beth of *Little Women* fame. *That* Beth died young, so as a child she never really inspired me. I certainly didn't want to identify with her, especially given that I'd been sickly, too, and had nearly died many times when I was young. Rather, it was the strong, independent Jo March, the heroine of that book, who really inspired me. She called to my essence, to step out and be fully who I was created to be. *Her* character dared me to be great, noble, and strong.

As a child, I was also vaguely aware of a rock song titled "Beth." The rock band Kiss sang it, but my parents didn't let me listen to rock music. We listened to classical and jazz music instead. So I wasn't really familiar with the trending rock songs of my time. Indeed, I wasn't trendy at all. I tended on the quieter, more introverted side, so the thought of a rock song bearing my name meant nothing to me. Neither did it relieve the pain of carrying such an uncommon name.

What was interesting was that my atheist (at best agnostic) parents were originally planning to name me Philippa—until they saw me. They looked at me and said, "She's not Philippa." And so I was a nameless baby for a while until they landed on Beth. Not Elizabeth, Bethany, or Elzabeth. Simply Beth.

So on this day when I was journaling, I became intrigued when God drew my attention to my name. I needed to understand what He was showing me by calling me My Beth on such a regular basis. After completing some research, the discovery I made was beautiful, affirming, and so very encouraging.

The meaning of my name is "house," or "dwelling place." It's a girl's name with Hebrew roots. Besides "house," it can also mean "pledged to God." I also discovered that Beth came from the letter *Bet*, the second letter of the Hebrew alphabet, and the first letter God began the Torah with. Apparently it's a very important letter in the Hebrew alphabet.

The shape of the letter *Bet* is in the shape of a house, but also the shape of a mouth. And so in calling me My Beth, God was speaking to me of being His house, His dwelling place, and His mouthpiece. I was a house and mouthpiece who took Him out onto the streets of

Melbourne. I was His dwelling place designed to carry the heart of God to the people there.

Now, theologically, that's true for us all. But by highlighting it in this quiet time with Him, He was showing me an element of my specific identity. And in that identity, He was revealing some of my purpose and design. It was and remains comforting knowledge. I had begun to step out for people as I went about my day, and here He was, affirming that I was His dwelling place as I did. From that place of intimacy, He spoke to me and showed me who I was to Him, in Him, and for Him. My understanding of my name has only grown from there, as He's expanded my purpose and spheres of influence.

So I encourage you, in your quiet time, to allow the Lord to draw your attention to things. Allow Him to invite you to explore truths about who you are and how He sees you. Explore the meaning of *your* name and any pet name He might have for you. Think about a biblical character with whom you most identify and let Him speak to you from there. From the place of intimacy we derive our kingdom identity, and that identity will point to our destiny, purpose, calling, and authority, much of which will be encapsulated in your name.

Look at the name God gave Himself. He called Himself "I Am." He is that He is. He was before, He's now, and He'll be forevermore. Similarly, Jesus is, was, and is to come. God has always existed, is existing, and will always exist. Indeed, simply put, God is because He exists outside time. He will always be the God of Abraham, the God of Isaac, and the God of Jacob. He's the God of the living, not the dead. Outside time, He exists on all time planes as we understand and know them. He simply is "I Am."

It is "I Am" who names His Son Jesus (Yeshua) because Jesus "will save his people from their sins" (Matthew 1:21). The name Jesus means "Jehovah saves" or "to deliver, to rescue." So contained within His name, Jesus' identity as Savior is encompassed, as is His purpose and His destiny—to be Savior and to save.

So who we say Jesus Christ is, is really the most important question we can ever answer. Because once settled, Jesus will reveal who heaven says we are. Now, please understand. God determined before time who we would be, what our giftings, callings, and purposes would entail. And those are irrevocable (Romans 11:29), so never fear you've missed anything. And of course when He called me My Beth, He was showing me He knew me, even before I was born. Formed in my mother's womb, He redirected my atheist parents to change the name they'd chosen. Even though they thought they would name me Philippa, He had it all in hand. Once I was born, He moved through them, speaking to their hearts: *She's not Philippa. Call her Beth, for she has a purpose and identity.*

A further memory He brought back to me was how the mother of a dear friend I had at twelve years of age would call me Bethel. To the best of my knowledge, she wasn't a Christian. She used the term as a form of Aussie endearment—we are a nation of nicknames. Crazy thing is, as the memory flooded back, I realized it pointed straight to my being the "house of God." As a twelve-year-old I was none the wiser, but when I journaled in my thirties, tears ran down my face. In that moment, I deeply appreciated how God had seen me all those years ago and had been speaking of my identity, purpose, and destiny throughout my life.

Just like William the ballet dancer I told you I prayed for in an earlier chapter, I didn't know God, yet He called me by name. He'd named me at birth through my unbelieving parents; He called me by name through an unbelieving woman, the mother of a friend; and here He was calling me by name as I journaled *My Beth*. Decades after I was born, I could recognize my purpose through my name, and with this revelation God gave me, He showed how He'd cared for me. It deeply encouraged me. I *felt* His affection and recognized His love present throughout my life. As the apple of His eye, *I* was His happy place. Ever since then my name has delighted me, for I know He called me by name, and with my name came my life's purpose and destiny.

WE MOVE FROM GLORY TO GLORY

I tell you how my time with God led me to knowing myself more intimately to encourage you. I can guarantee this will also happen for you.

To yada with God will draw you deep into your design, and from there you will joyfully go forth.

In discovering who Jesus is, we discover who we are too. However, this won't stop there. The revelation of who Jesus is continues throughout our lives, as does the revelation of who we're called to be. Remember that "we all, who with unveiled faces contemplate the Lord's glory, are being transformed into his image with ever-increasing glory, which comes from the Lord, who is the Spirit" (2 Corinthians 3:18). Recognizing who Jesus is will open the door to discover our most true selves and with that, our purpose and kingdom destiny. He will call you by name to come to Him, and He will then call you by name to reveal your true self. Spend time with Him, get to know Him, and as you do, you'll come to know yourself and see that you truly are His happy place!

QUESTIONS TO CONTEMPLATE

1. What is the meaning of your birth names (first, middle, and last), married name, and even nickname? Take time with God to explore what He has to say about the meanings of your names and how they might connect to your identity and purpose in Him.
2. What biblical or historical characters do you relate to in this season? Were you named after any biblical or historical characters? What is the meaning of their name? With God, explore whether they are a clue to your purpose and destiny. Look at who they were in history, what their role was, the impact they had, and how they're known today. Even characters whose lives didn't end well had God's promises within them. Each character God identifies is an invitation into a conversation about what promises within those people you also carry.
3. Look up the meaning of the names of biblical characters you relate to or that God highlights to you. Then ask Him

how the meaning of those names might point to your own purpose, destiny, and kingdom design. Journal about what you discover.

RESPONSE TO THE REVELATION

- **Action Step 1:** Take some time with God each day and ask Him to show you what else He might say to you about your names and kingdom identity. Journal what you discover. This is not a one-off conversation but an ongoing dialogue about who you are and who you're becoming.
- **Action Step 2:** Throughout your week, be aware of people's names. Ask them if they know the meaning of their name. If they don't, look it up for them. Ask God for a word of encouragement for those people based on the meaning of their name. Ask Him how He sees them and what He would like you to say to them about their name, purpose, and destiny.

LET'S PRAY

Father, thank You for calling me by name and that my name has a meaning and a purpose. I ask You to speak to me through my name and show me all You have purposed for me within it. I also ask for any new names You might call me in this season or in a season to come. Highlight any other names You might have for me so I will understand my identity in You with greater clarity and insight. And last, help me see who You want to be for me as I choose to step into the identity You have for me. In Jesus' mighty name I pray, amen.

11

LOVERS AND WORKERS

"Very truly I tell you, the Son can do nothing by himself;
he can do only what he sees his Father doing,
because whatever the Father does the Son also does."
John 5:19

WHEN I FIRST MET MY husband, we spent every moment we could together. Enjoying each other's company, learning of each other's likes and dislikes, and growing in understanding of what pleased the other we grew closer and more secure in our relationship. With commitment came marriage, and so the journey continues today, some thirty-plus years later.

Many mention how Andrew watches me with love in his eyes. There's a genuine joy as he celebrates who I am and who I'm becoming. It's so apparent that people comment, and it's been a witness to others—even pre-believers—of a kingdom marriage. Naturally, this affection flows from me to him, too, but keep with me as I draw out the analogy.

My husband observes our children with a similar delight. His eyes shine as he watches them grow, and with a father's pleasure, he nurtures them. Teaching through example, but also through loving encouragement, he guides their way into adulthood. He wants our children to find their purpose, their passion, and their place—to thrive in all they do. Naturally, he fully expects them to mature into functioning, healthy adults.

If the children or I truly desire something, Andrew will help us achieve it. As his wife, I've learned to hold his heart gently, understanding what might wound his soul, and through time spent together, I know what touches his heart most. Privy to his heart's desires, I in turn choose to assist him with his dreams as well. I don't do so because he controls me or demands it of me but because I love him. His dreams have become my dreams, and my dreams have become his.

In the same way, you are God's beloved. You are the bride of Christ and a child of God.[1] *You* are God's happy place. His eyes fill with love as He watches you, and in the secret place of intimacy, He nurtures, teaches, encourages, and inspires. He listens to your needs and even your wants, and He cherishes the sound of your voice. As the lover of your soul, God yearns to be with you. He calls you to cease striving, to rest in His arms and *be* with him (Psalm 46:10).

Isaiah 62:5 puts it beautifully: "As a young man marries a young woman, so will your Builder marry you; as a bridegroom rejoices over his bride, so will your God rejoice over you." God rejoices over you as you rest in the arms of Jesus. And yet there's more to do than simply gaze at His face, for from the place of divine love, drawn by the desires of His heart, you will want to meet *His* heart's desires as well. And His heart's desires are His Father's heart desires. Together with Jesus, inspired by the Holy Spirit, you will desire to be about the Father's delight—that is, to be about His business.

WE ARE DRAWN INTO LOVE'S EMBRACE

As lovers of God, we are each called into His embrace. He draws us deep *into* Him, where we find our unique place *with* Him in our God space. Love bids us to linger, and as in any relationship, such time spent causes greater intimacy.

Pause for a moment. Intimacy. We gaze into Him and He will

"into-me-see." And as we gaze back and forth, we discover we are God's happy place. Love's purpose revealed, our hearts will meld as one in the deep place of consecrated unity. He draws us into His embrace so we might understand the truth of the statement Jesus made in John 14:20: "You are in me, and I am in you." But to abide and never emerge was not the plan. God's purpose is not for us to cave dwell forevermore with Him, but neither is it to go out and do work alone. Rather, there is an ebb and flow. We "ebb," or pull away from the world, drawn into Love's embrace. But then from that place of intimacy we "flow," or go into all the world to make disciples.[2] Disciples who will lean on Him and learn from Him as we have done, in the secret place.

FROM LOVE'S EMBRACE, WE GO

Through abiding in the Lord, our hearts will meld with His, for to enter the place of consecration with the Trinity so imbues us with the Father's heart that we can't help but be about the Father's business. However, so many miss the first step and run deep into performance mode, striving for an acceptance already won. Others desire to only sit at the feet of the Father and choose to never venture forth. While both are valuable in themselves, I suggest a better way is the simple melding of the two. This involves a time when we are simply with God, and from that place we flow.

So there is an ebb (a retreat time) and a flow (an outward time). Both involve a constant awareness of God, but the outworking looks different. In the flow, we *go* while in constant dialogue with Him throughout the day. If we can hold that tension of ebb and flow (and also constant dialogue or awareness of Him), we will naturally be about the Father's business. Because in both the ebb and flow He will guide our steps, encourage our ways, and point to those He wants us to reach.

IT'S NOT MARY OR MARTHA BUT BOTH MARY *AND* MARTHA

In the story of Mary and Martha, we see a beautiful analogy of the ebb and flow. Having invited Jesus into their home, Martha becomes busy preparing things *for* Jesus while her sister Mary sits at His feet. Then she asks Jesus, "Lord, don't you care that my sister has left me to do the work by myself? Tell her to help me!" (Luke 10:39–40).

We all know Mary chose well because Jesus commends her for choosing to sit at His feet: "'Martha, Martha,' the Lord answered, 'you are worried and upset about many things, but few things are needed—or indeed only one. Mary has chosen what is better, and it will not be taken away from her'" (10:41–42).

Though many have used this Scripture as an excuse to remain gazing into the eyes of Jesus while refusing to rise and do anything, I suggest that Mary simply chose well *in the moment*. We see Martha "distracted by all the preparations that had to be made" (10:40) when Jesus was there to *be with* them. In her busyness, she couldn't sit still, cease her striving, and take advantage of His visit. It was clearly time for her to get to know Him better. As we've discussed, sometimes we're called to be still and know that He is God (Psalm 46:10).

Here, in the quiet moment, we will feel His love. He sees us, but more importantly, *we* can see Him. And, of course, Jesus said, "Anyone who has seen me has seen the Father" (John 14:9). So when we sit at the feet of Jesus, as Mary did, we're sitting at the feet of the Father, for Jesus and the Father are one and the same. They are separate yet one. And here we realize how God adores us, how much He approves of us, and how we are His happy place!

However, if we're to remain sitting at the feet of Jesus, we would become, as some would say, so heavenly focused that we would be of no earthly good. In this time, we learn God won't love us any more or any less than He already does, because He adores us exactly as we are. We don't need to *do* a thing to be loved, and yet like any good father, God wants us to grow into maturity, and this growth requires a choice toward action on our behalf.

In this time of being the lover of Jesus, we become imbued with

His love. The more time we spend with Him, the more we take on His heart's desires. We become saturated with His heart for others as He loves the world to Himself. In this place, we can't help but care for the thing, or rather the *who,* resting upon His heart. We also learn He created us with a purpose in mind, "for we are God's masterpiece . . . [created] anew in Christ Jesus, so we can do the good things He planned for us long ago" (Ephesians 2:10 NLT). As we understand how much He adores us, we will also appreciate that we're called to fulfill His plans and purposes for our lives, which is simply to be about the Father's business.

WE ARISE TO GO WITH JESUS

Though we're called to spend time alone with Jesus, sometimes He'll say, "Arise, my darling, my beautiful one, come with me" (Song of Songs 2:10). These are times when we must go forth from that place of being still. As we venture forth, we "arise" with Him and go. We are both lovers and workers designed to flow with the love of heaven, inviting all to come meet the lover of their souls.

In John 11:1–44, Martha and Mary's brother, Lazarus, falls ill and dies. Just after his death we see Martha go out to meet Jesus:[3] "When Martha heard that Jesus was coming, *she went out to meet him* [with great expectation], *but Mary stayed at home.* 'Lord,' Martha said to Jesus, 'if you had been here, my brother would not have died. But I know that even now God will give you whatever you ask'" (11:20–22, emphasis added).

Martha, the sister who gets things done, hears Jesus is coming and goes out to meet him. In comparison, Mary stays home. It's Martha who declares her faith in Him, stating, "Even now, God will give you whatever you ask" (11:22). And it's Martha who goes back for her sister Mary, who has stayed sitting in her grief, to tell her, "The Teacher is here . . . and is asking for you" (11:28).

Martha knows where Jesus is and goes out to meet Him. In doing so, she receives a deeper revelation as she seeks Him in her need. She knows He has resurrection power within, and with a statement of great faith, she greets Him, saying she knows God will grant Him whatever He asks. Beautifully, Jesus responds confirming her hopes and grants her even deeper insight into who He truly is:

> Jesus said to her, "Your brother will rise again."
>
> Martha answered, "I know he will rise again in the resurrection at the last day."
>
> Jesus said to her, "I am the resurrection and the life. The one who believes in me will live, even though they die; and whoever lives by believing in me will never die. Do you believe this?"
>
> "Yes, Lord," she replied, "I believe that you are the Messiah, the Son of God, who is to come into the world."
>
> After she had said this, she went back and called her sister Mary aside. "The Teacher is here," she said, "and is asking for you." (John 11:23–28)

It's Martha who draws Mary back to Jesus. And while Mary rises immediately upon hearing her sister call for her, she wasn't looking for what Jesus was doing at that moment. She'd remained home, where she'd encountered Him previously, but He wasn't there anymore. He was busy being about His Father's business. While Jesus is active, like a "Martha" we can join Him by His side and call others to join Him as well. Remaining in the place of a past encounter and refusing to look to where Jesus might be heading, we can miss the place of our greatest miracle.

Sometimes we need to sit at the feet of Jesus, but other times we go out to meet Him, wherever He is. We join Him in being about the Father's business, and in this instance, the Father's business was to raise Lazarus. We are all called to be "Marys" sometimes, but at other times we need to be "Marthas," actively seeking solutions—for ourselves and for others too. As we're actively engaging with Jesus in what He's doing in our day, we'll point the way to the "Marys," helping them meet Jesus where He is, to join Him in what He's doing too. We must meet Him as He goes, and when He goes, for He's always about the Father's business.

Remember, Jesus tells us that "the Son can do nothing by himself; he can do only what he sees His Father doing, because whatever the Father does the Son also does" (John 5:19). He says, "I do nothing on my own but speak just what the Father has taught me" (John 8:28), and He affirms His focus when He says, "The words I say to you I do not speak on my own authority. Rather, it is the Father, living in me, who is doing his work" (John 14:10).

From a young age, Jesus knew He was to be about His Father's business (Luke 2:49). It was His way, His lifestyle. Jesus went and lived always about His Father's business, representing God to the world, reconciling the world through Himself, and showing us what God personified looked like as He lived His life. We're called to be lovers like Mary and workers like Martha, for we are ultimately called to love God with all our heart, soul, mind, and strength (Mark 12:30) as we go about the Father's business. For Jesus Himself said to us all, "Very truly I tell you, whoever believes in me will do the works I have been doing, and they will do even greater things than these, because I am going to the Father" (John 14:12).

THE SIGN OF MATURITY—BEING ABOUT THE FATHER'S BUSINESS

As in any healthy relationship, we grow to understand it's not "all about me." And a sign of growing maturity is to understand that our relationship with Jesus is an invitation into the family business, with God as our chief executive officer. It's not simply about sitting in that quiet place and *being with* God, asking to be cared for, and calling for favor and blessings only for us. But neither is it only about "getting the work of ministry done." God seeks those who know how to receive love and how to love others as they joyfully go about His kingdom business.

Like any great parent, God wants His children to grow up. His desire is for lovers to be so imbued with His love that they become workers *with* Him, not *for* him. Our relationship with God is not only about me or about you but about the Father and His heart for the nations as He calls them home to be by His Son's side. He wants as many as possible to come to the wedding banquet. True maturity is to understand that it's all about the heart of the Father. It's all about the Father's business. It's a family business constantly looking to expand. And as with any family business, sometimes we lay down our own agendas because we love Him and choose to co-labor with Him to see His dreams fulfilled. We are a "Mary" who sits at the feet of the Father and then steps out and flows into "Martha" activity. And that activity will include others too.

GOD IS GOOD STORY: ABOUT THE FATHER'S BUSINESS

I dropped my son at school and was heading home when I had a fleeting thought: *Head up to the local hardware store and buy a padlock for your new gate.*

Odd, I thought. *I'm just around the corner from home. I'll go home first to collect a piece of pipe I need to return to the store, and then I'll head up as directed.*

Although I'd recognized this thought as God speaking to me, in *my* wisdom, I kept driving toward home. It made more sense to collect the pipe I needed to return and *then* go. It would save me a second trip to the same place that day. But then I checked my plan with God and knew immediately that I was not to go home first. I was to go straight to the hardware store—*now*.

Odd, I thought again as I drove past my home. *But what have I got to lose in listening and obeying as I go?* I pondered further, and wondered who or what I would encounter at the store when I got there.

I found a parking space quickly and headed straight into the store. Immediately, I saw a friend from church who worked there, standing at the door giving directions to customers.

I smiled at her and said, "Oh, you must be the reason I came. You're a blessing for me to see."

We had a brief chat before I found what I needed, and as I made my way to the checkout, she caught me and suggested I let her buy me a coffee. I hesitated. With so much to do, I wasn't sure I could manage the time. I was already behind on *my* agenda with this extra stop-off for God. Seeing me hesitate, she said, "Look, no pressure. I know you're very busy."

"No, no, I'm just checking with the Holy Spirit to see what He says. I *am* very busy, but He wants me to stop, and *I* would love to have a coffee with you. Thank you."

We chatted over a cuppa, and it *was* lovely. I felt blessed to just be with a friend.

With her break time finished, my friend returned to her post by the store door and I stood in line to pay for my padlock, thinking about my day and the jobs I needed to complete. When it was my turn to check out, I looked at the woman serving me, and in an instant I knew I needed to offer to pray.

After paying for my purchase, I said to her, "This may sound strange, but I'm a Christian, and I have an overwhelming sense that I need to offer to pray for you. Is there anything specific I can pray?"

The woman looked at me, shook a little, and then tearing up, she said, "Yes. There is something you can pray for me. There is . . . but . . . I . . ."

I knew not to push for details. It was clearly private, and she was obviously overwhelmed.

"It's okay," I said. "You don't need to tell me. God knows the details. I will bless you, but He knows what you need, which is why He wanted me to ask if you needed prayer."

She nodded, but then someone else came up behind me to check out. I stood back. "I'll wait," I said, smiling.

The woman finished serving the person behind me, and yet another person came forward to check out. They seemed to completely overlook the other available checkout station. But I stood and waited some more, and as she finished with that one, yet *another* person came, and then yet another!

I continued to stand, waiting. It happens so often. I'll offer to pray, and suddenly the checkout aisles fill with customers. The cashier will often seem a little nervous with me waiting, but I know to wait, looking relaxed, even if I don't *feel* relaxed. In fact, so often I feel very awkward as I wait. But I've learned to be patient, knowing that the time to pray will come. If I can just stand my ground, I *will* fulfill my assignment.

I quietly prayed for an opening, for the flow of people to slow, and with a little patience, it came. I walked back to the register and told her my name. She then gave me hers—I'll call her Hannah—and I took her hand and prayed. I leaned into the Father's heart for her and prayed a blessing and for favor, and because I sensed she needed wisdom, I prayed for wisdom in the pathways forward. I prayed knowing God knew what her needs were, and I declared He would meet them all.

As I did, Hannah's eyes filled with tears.

No profound "knowing" or prophetic words came to me that pierced the situation. I just felt a deep sense of compassion for her, in whatever place she found herself in. She wanted to remain private, and I honored her in that, as did God, by not giving me any more insight other than what I already knew. In fact, it was enough that I offered to pray, and she accepted the prayer. I knew it was enough for the heavenly hosts to move on her behalf and release God's goodness into her situation. Prayer always effects change.

I finished, sensing I was to bless Hannah with something I call "the Father's blessing." I knew I needed to kiss her forehead and bless her as I did. It's a blessing I'm sometimes directed to give, and I try to respond in obedience whenever I feel prompted. I told her God was very pleased with her, that He loved her. She shook as I spoke these words over her. I then asked her if I could kiss her forehead. This completely undid her, and she shook her head and sobbed.

"It's okay," I said, knowing not to push it. Instead, I simply kissed my finger and placed it upon her head.

"Thank you for letting me pray for you," I whispered. Then I walked away as the next customer came forward. Hannah simply wiped her tears away as she tried to compose herself.

On my way out, I once again encountered my friend, still at the door. She knew what was going on. She'd seen me pray for others in that store and at coffee shops too. I suggested she keep an eye out for Hannah.

"I'll look out for her," she promised.

I left knowing Hannah was in excellent hands because my friend would look out for her, as would God. And as I left, I said to God, *Well, that was an interesting morning. I saw a friend, had a cup of coffee and a lovely chat, and had an encounter waiting for me. Thank You.*

I smiled at Him, feeling my deep love for Him, and as I did, I felt His deep love for me. I was His lover, but I was His worker too.

It had been a good morning.

As I drove home, I realized that had I'd rushed home instead of going to the hardware store for a padlock, I would have missed my friend. In missing her, I would not have had the cuppa I didn't have time for. I would also have missed Hannah at the checkout because she wasn't working there when I was originally heading out. My friend would also have missed seeing the encounter, and she wouldn't have known to care for Hannah. God had it all timed to perfection.

Had I listened to my logic (had I "logic'd it," as my family say) and stopped at home first, I might have become distracted and left it too late. I might never have engaged with the woman God wanted to reach with His love. Indeed, I may not have made it to the hardware store at all. If I had insisted on my agenda, rather than checking in with God that morning, had I failed to recognize the fleeting idea as potentially being a "God idea," I would have missed it.

Instead, I'm glad I listened. Through practice over time, I've learned to check with God when such inconvenient or strange ideas pop into my head from "nowhere." Sometimes these ideas seem crazy, but they're not so crazy when you work it out and see what happens in the end. These God ideas are an invitation for us to co-labor with Him, to work with Him in "the family business." I've so often missed it, but through missing it and letting the Holy Spirit teach me in loving-kindness, I now miss these moments far less than I once did. I had nothing to lose to follow the prompting, and if I got it wrong, I knew my obedience was still pleasing to Him, for God is my audience of one.

So often God will have us stop for "the one" as we go about our day. If we recognize the moment and respond to His voice, even when the idea makes no sense according to *our* agenda, He will give us the privilege of co-creating with Him. In so following God's agenda rather than my own, Hannah now knows God cares for her, loves her, sees her, and is real!

HE LOVES FIRST, WE LOVE IN RESPONSE, AND TOGETHER WE GO

We are God's lovers foremost, but we're His workers too. It's first lover, then worker. And from there it becomes *both* lover *and* worker but never lover *or* worker. That's because, dare I say, I doubt you can be imbued with God and not care about what His heart desires.

In its simplest form, we choose to be still and practice His presence. This is a precious time for you and Him to cherish and live with each other in joyful, quiet solitude. From there we go, looking to see what God is up to as we do life *with* Him. I believe this includes stopping for the one as invited by the Holy Spirit while intentionally fulfilling our kingdom purpose and destiny.

There's a constant flow of conversation from God to you and from you to Him. You're in a relationship—like I am with Andrew and Andrew is with me, like Andrew is with our children and our children are with Andrew. Andrew loves me as his wife, and together we step forth into the world to achieve *both* our heart's desires. I take Andrew out with me and introduce him to the world. I don't keep him hidden. And similarly, Andrew loves our children and desires them to grow up into full maturity, to step into all they're designed to do. They engage with him as they grow and mention him to the world around them too.

If a good parent wants good things for their child, including maturation, how much more so our perfect heavenly Father? (Matthew 7:11). He delights in us while desiring only the best for us. We're each His happy place—our photo is on His fridge. His loving gaze is always upon us, He whispers sweet nothings to us, and yet He wants us to grow up so we might co-reign with His Son, Jesus.

While it's lovely to sit and behold His face, to gaze into the eyes of Jesus is not all you're designed for. Neither are you to only go out and perform good deeds *for* God and His kingdom. No, it's not one *or* the other, but one *and* the other. You are His lover *and* worker, magnificently created by a loving God who holds you in His gaze as He calls forth the deep things He set you upon this earth to complete. He brought you into being to be loved *by Him* while you co-labor (or rather, co-create) *with* Him. He cast His eye upon your design before the dawning of time and gave you a purpose, a plan, a people, and a place.

There is work to do, and to do *your* designated work is to live in the place of your greatest fulfillment and joy. All the while you remain His happy place, as the friction of life causes you to grow into your truest self. It's from the chamber of His love that you must step out, for both lover and worker is your call. As you love Him, you'll delight in being about the Father's business, for in that place is your God-given design.

QUESTIONS TO CONTEMPLATE

1. When have you been acutely aware of Jesus being by your side as you've stepped into what you believed God wanted you to do? What was that like? Was there a sense of delight, ease, or joy? If not, what did you feel? Journal your thoughts and insights.
2. Can you identify God-created opportunities for you to step into your design and purpose? Even if you're not sure about your purpose, journal what God brings to mind.
3. When have you felt ill-equipped or even completely unqualified and yet seen God move through your life? What does that say to you about who He is for you? What does that say about how ready you need to be to take the first step toward your kingdom purpose and design?

RESPONSE TO THE REVELATION

- **Action Step 1:** Each day spend time with God and ask Him to identify your current spheres of influence. We all have them even if it's at a local store, gas station, barbershop, or hair salon. Thinking about what you've learned so far, inquire of God how you can step forth into your immediate spheres of influence and be about the Father's business. Ask Him what that might look like for you. Journal what you discover.
- **Action Step 2:** Throughout your week, stay aware of the Holy Spirit being with you as you go about your days. Invite God to highlight what He'd like you to do, where He'd like you to go, and what His agenda might be. Be open to changing your day to accommodate what's on the Father's heart. Journal your adventures and share them with someone you trust.

LET'S PRAY

Father, thank You that I am Your beloved, that I'm Your happy place. As I sink deep into the knowledge of Your love for me, please show me what You have purposed for me to do to also be about Your family business. I ask that You highlight people to meet, places to go, and projects to be involved in. I ask for blueprints and plans for my life ahead—and for clarity in timing and ways. Thank You for the privilege of co-laboring with Your Son, Jesus, and the Holy Spirit as I engage with what You have placed in my hands to do.

Let me always remember to sit at Your feet, like Mary, and to rise up and meet You, like Martha. May I have the privilege to call others by Your side as You build. Help me love You first and then be about Your business. In Jesus' mighty name I pray, amen.

12

GOD'S LOVE NEVER ENDS

There is a river whose streams make glad the city of God.
Psalm 46:4

IN A WORLD where acceptance rests on performance and love has conditions, the idea of a love that never ends is difficult to grasp. Social media, advertising, the news, current affairs, community groups, and for some of us even our churches, friends, and families scream *Conform or I will block you, abandon you, or disown you.*

However, as children of God, we inhabit and serve a different kingdom—a kingdom from which a river of love flows direct from the throne room of heaven (Ezekiel 47). So imbued with the love of God it's beyond our comprehension. This flowing river is the Holy Spirit, who flows ever outward toward all humankind. The flow of the river is counterintuitive. Ezekiel describes how it deepens the farther it runs from its source and so it is different to our way of thinking. It ever reaches into crevices of darkness, where love seems not to exist. Its essence is so profound that it causes change in all those it encounters. Offering eternal reconciliation with God through the gift of Jesus Christ, the river brings healing and life wherever it flows.

Referred to by Jesus as "living waters" when He spoke with the woman at the well (John 4:1–26), the Holy Spirit flows as a source of constant love toward us, takes up residence within us, and in turn flows forth from those of us willing to go. Jesus said, "When you drink the water I give you, it becomes a gushing fountain of the Holy Spirit, flooding you with endless life!" (John 4:14 TPT). We become free, like the woman at the well, and can take Him forth into our community wherever we live. As we flow with these living waters, we become the streams running from the river that make the city of God glad (Psalm 46:4). We bubble forth with His goodness directly from the waters, and as we do, we partake of God's joy in the task at hand. We are His happy place, and He delights as we step into all He has in store.

But what if we choose not to flow at the sound of His voice? What if we choose to disobey? Will God still love us? Will His love truly never end? Will He love me, will He love you, if we refuse to move forward into our kingdom design and destiny and be about the Father's business?

In theory, we should all know the answer to these questions. God's extravagant love for us, toward us, and within us is endless. His love is clearly evidenced by the gift of His Son, Jesus Christ, before time. Love is why He created us, love was the solution He provided for us, in love He became us, and through love the price was paid. So yes, categorically I can say that God's love for you will never end, and *because* He loves us so, He will constantly invite us to fully embrace His ways. God is love, and love always looks for the highest good for the sake of those loved. As any good father, God guides, protects, and provides discipline too, for of course He wants His children to grow. While always protecting our free will, God will help us become all He's designed us to be. So we choose to either flow in response to God's love, *with* God's love, and make the city of God glad, or we choose not to. Either way His love will never end.

The journey into maturity is conceptually simple. Luxuriate in who He is, and we'll fall deeply in love with Him. As we do, we'll grow confident in who God is and who He says we are too. As we rest in the knowledge of His nature and character, we deepen our understanding that doing what He asks will not only lead to our greatest place and joy here on earth but cause us to mature and grow. In recognizing and responding to His voice, we fall deeper in love with Him *as* we see His ways manifest all around us. We impact the world with His love, and so the words spoken by Jesus, "If you love me, keep my commands" (John 14:15) make sense and are effortless to fulfill.

Easy, right? Yep . . . and nope! While, again, this is conceptually simple, obedience and with it growth isn't always easy. The process of maturation isn't straightforward nor plain because it so often requires an uncomfortable refining. It's simply not fun. However, whether or not we engage with God's plans, we can always be sure His love for us will never fail nor end. We are always His happy place, but we don't always make the city of God glad. His gladness comes as we flow in what we're purposed to do in a given time and season. It's not performance driven but delight in seeing us flow into the fullness of our intended design.

LOVE GUIDES AND ENCOURAGES THE BEST

The opportunities God provides us to step into our true identity are endless. Using life to refine, God corrects as we grow, serving as proof of His love for us as His children. His discipline (teaching, training, and direction) is clear proof of our adoption into His family (Hebrews 12:8). Paul tells us that God will meet all our needs "according to the riches" of His glory in His Son, Jesus Christ (Philippians 4:19), and sometimes those needs include His firm guidance. Such guidance should never be seen as anything but encouragement to choose His ways over our own.

In my walk with God, the Holy Spirit has strongly encouraged me to cease behaviors counterproductive to my God-given identity and hence my God-given purpose and design. Many moments I've had to step back from my first instinct while He asked me not to engage with old habits and belief patterns. When this occurs, He strips away strongholds of thought, and past wounds are exposed.

These moments are an invitation into God's arms to be made whole. We heal in His presence. Although never perfect, I do my best to respond to God's promptings, and I know it delights Him as I incline my heart toward Him and His ways. In being willing, I know I please Him. In being willing, you please Him too. This is when we flow with the river of God and become streams that make the city of God glad. We are His happy place!

Let me share a story that might help you understand.

GOD IS GOOD STORY: AND HE PLAYED FOOTBALL THAT SATURDAY

It was mid-winter as I drove to collect my daughter from school. There was an icy drizzle, and as such it was a miserable day for anyone to be walking without adequate clothing and protection.

I was nearly at school when I saw a stay-at-home dad (parent to one of my daughter's friends) walking to the school in the rain. I'll call him Luke. Luke wore shorts and flip-flops or sneakers all year, and his demeanor caused many a mommy tongue to wag in gossip. A diamond in the rough, he called a spade a spade, but regardless, I liked him. I pulled over and offered him a ride.

Luke thought for a moment, then said, "I'd normally say no, but on this day, I'll accept because I have a really sore knee."

We rode the short distance to school, chatting as we went, and I asked him about his knee.

"It's an old injury that requires a knee reconstruction," he replied, sighing in resignation.

Feeling God's love as we walked into the schoolyard, I knew I needed to offer to pray, but I didn't know how since I would be in front of all the moms at school pickup. But I'd received a very clear picture in my mind's eye of what the prayer would look like. I'd recently learned that God sometimes gives us a mental picture of how He wants us to pray to release a healing. In the picture, I was kneeling on the ground in front of Luke, with my hand placed on his bare knee as I prayed. With that picture in mind, I offered to pray, hoping he'd say no.

"I don't believe in any of that stuff," he said. "I'm an atheist, but you can give it a go if you like. If it works, it'll be great. I'll be able to play footy this Saturday, but I doubt it'll work." (In Australia, we play Australian Rules Football, called "Aussie Rules" or "footy."[1])

I panicked a little when he accepted. I didn't want to kneel before Luke the way I'd seen in my imagination. The ground was wet, and he was a man wearing shorts. I felt it was inappropriate for me to kneel with my hand on his bare knee. And again, all the other moms were milling around waiting for their kids to come out of school! So in my "wisdom," I placed my hand discreetly upon his shoulder and prayed. However, as I prayed I heard a strong rebuke in my spirit. It wasn't nasty or mean, but it *was* firm. I heard God say, *Stop being such a prude! I showed you how to pray, now do it. Get on your knees and pray.*

I took a deep breath, focusing on the fact that Luke might receive healing, and explained I needed to place my hand on his knee.

"Do whatever you want," he said back.

So I knelt on the cold ground, and as the dampness soaked through my jeans and the mothers watched with sideways glances, I prayed. Feeling vulnerable and embarrassed, still on my knees, I looked up at Luke.

"Do you feel anything?"

"I can feel heat," he said.

So I kept praying.

"Move your knee around," I said after a little more prayer. "Test it out."

Luke did and said he felt some relief. So I prayed again, remaining on my knees. But once I felt I was done, I stood and asked him to try it out yet again. He bent his knee back and forth and moved it all around.

"All the pain has gone!" he said, surprised.

"Jump on it!" I insisted, and I jumped up and down on the spot to show him how.

Luke jumped up and down with me, and a look of amazement crossed his face. "There's no more pain! I would not have believed it, but I felt the heat. It's amazing. I might even be wrong about this stuff . . ." He looked puzzled as the truth of what had occurred sunk in.

Delighted but still feeling awkward, I got on with collecting my daughter and headed home.

I saw Luke the following week and asked, "How did you get on last weekend?"

He looked straight at me with absolute joy-filled delight and said, "I played my game of footy last Saturday!" and he grinned from ear to ear.

Luke *experienced* the love of God. Clearly God had no concerns about blessing him, even though he didn't believe in God. Regardless of his faith, or lack thereof, God chose to heal him for a football match that many might say was trivial. The point is, it mattered to Luke, so it mattered to God. In a moment, he discovered God might be real and even cared for him personally. God met his felt need, the experience of which shifted his mindset and heart to the possible existence of a loving God.

Luke was God's happy place, and God wanted him to know it, so He showed it through taking care of the minute details of an unbelieving man's life. God's never-ending love flowed, and a closed heart opened to a possibility not considered before.

GOD'S LOVE REFINES AND HONES

As you lean into God's presence in your life, His never-ending love will refine you. The correction I received was a firm rebuke, but it was kind. I was God's happy place as He taught me how His ways will always work for good. Indeed, I believe my prayer became a witness to those who watched, but regardless, God's love affected my friend Luke.

Little did I know that the effect would leave a love imprint that ultimately saved a life. For when we release God's love in obedience, not only is it about us learning God's ways, or us growing into who we are, or about making the city of God glad, but it teaches and encourages those who receive His love through us too. *They* become changed and new. God's love for you, encouraging you to trust Him and grow, will never end. But so, too, His love for them never ends! He wants us to grow into maturity, to understand that *His* ways work for the best in our lives. But He also wants us to understand that His ways work as He flows through us to impact the community around us with His love.

Perhaps a year later, without shame, Luke explained to me how he'd hated an elderly neighbor, and late on a cold mid-winter's day, he'd heard the man faintly calling from his garden. Luke suspected and later verified that the man had fallen and couldn't get back up.

"I seriously considered leaving him there to die!" he said to my horror. He knew his neighbor was frail enough that he would surely die of exposure. Brutally honest in the retelling, Luke added, "I'd be done with him once and for all!" As he listened to his neighbor's feeble calls for help, he considered his options. But then he had what he described as a "battle." He said it was as if he had an angel sitting on one shoulder and a devil on the other. The devil told him to let the man die, but the angel made him think of me. I was symbolic of God for him; I symbolized a river of love. He was aware of the love he encountered in the healing of his knee and in many other interactions we'd had.

Luke said, "You'd be proud of me. I let the angel win!" He went to the elderly man's aid, and upon calling for an ambulance, the medics told him he'd undoubtedly saved the man's life. He said that without our chats and all he'd experienced in our interactions over time, he would have happily left the man for dead.

While you may find this shocking (I know I sure did), I want you to know that responding to God's instructions and guidance is more than just dying to self. The author of Hebrews says, "Now all discipline seems to be painful at the time, yet later it will produce a transformation of character, bringing a harvest of righteousness and peace to those who yield to it" (Hebrews 12:11 TPT).

God's endless love is for us, but also for those we'll reach. His love can include a firm reproach, a hefty command, or even a time-out to reflect. These moments are never to punish, nor to cease communication. God doesn't play games, nor does He give us the silent treatment. Rather, His discipline is to help us grow into all we can be so we can step into all we're called to do, bringing both us and the city of God the most joy. We must all remember, too, that the harvest will go well beyond ourselves or even the ones we pray for, because, again, the river of God gets deeper the farther from the throne room it flows.

Love reached through this grouchy man who had tasted and seen God's never-ending love for himself. In the flow of living (loving) waters released from me to Luke, his heart was changed, and Love won out! He chose to save his neighbor's life, and my friend was changed forever more.

GOD DISCIPLINES HIS CHILDREN

In Proverbs 3:12 we learn that a loving father will discipline a child he loves and accepts. God delights in us all and wants only the best for us. As a good Father, He desires His children to grow into all they're destined for, and He uses correction to help steer our way. Somehow, in our humanity, we've perceived God's discipline as harsh and punitive, whereas the word translated as "discipline" in Hebrews 12:5–6 and 11 excludes such ideas. Rather than invoking the idea of an angry parent "disciplining," or punishing us, for poor behavior, the original passage suggests something else. The word used in the original is the Hebrew word *mûsâr*, meaning "discipline," "chastening," or "correction," but the word's meaning doesn't extend to any form of punitive punishment.[2] So while many of us might think of God's discipline as punitive, it simply is not. He doesn't punish us. Rather, He teaches, guides, and corrects because He loves us, because we are His happy place.

I think The Passion Translation of the Bible catches it best in Proverbs 3:11–12: "My child, when the Lord God speaks to you, never take his words lightly, and never be upset when he corrects you. For the Father's discipline comes only from his passionate love and pleasure for you." Even when it seems like His correction is harsh, it's still better than any father on earth gives to his child.

So the journey with God is really one of being guided and taught by a loving Father. He loves us completely, and as we spend time with Him, we become fully immersed in Him. He disciplines, encourages, and kindly rebukes, giving us boundaries for our own good. He trains us as we go, and He does so because He loves us as His beloved children in whom He is well pleased! We are His happy place, and we cause Him great delight as we flow. We are streams flowing from the river that itself flows directly from the throne room of God. And as we flow in the fullness of our kingdom identity, doing what we were born to do, we cause great joy in the city of God. But regardless of how we flow, His love for us will never end!

Of course, in the story about my rough and rugged friend, God guided, encouraged, and taught me, and I grew. I learned more about myself and about Him too. There were places I needed freedom, such as freedom from the fear of man and the fear of failure to name but two. I learned more about the perfection of God's ways and how His endless love will always flow. He disciplined (or discipled) me, and I grew. Kneeling while praying was a simple thing to do, and yet so challenging. But I was privileged to witness the effect of those living waters. It was miraculous. His teaching has never stopped, and my journey continues to this day. I've since learned to hear His rebuke and correction through the lens of *His* love, not through my own earthly lenses of criticism, judgment, and conditional love.

So while His love never ends, our willingness to obey (to respond to His voice) becomes a doorway into deeper intimacy, but we choose. Works alone are not what He desires (Ephesians 2:8–9). Rather, He seeks our willingness to be with Him, to know Him, and for Him to know us. As we go, we naturally respond to the heartbeat of heaven, and it's in *this* place, most of all, that we discover He adores us—we are His happy place.

But regardless, His love will never end, and because it will never end, He gives us endless opportunities to say yes to His plans for our lives. These choices will always help us grow. To fully catch the truth of this is liberating. No matter what, we can never lose His love. His love is a done deal, regardless of when we might have fallen short of other's expectations or our own. That surety of His love becomes our foundation from which all life flows. It gives us a security to know we can step forth, "fail," and try again without risk of losing the Father's heart. Indeed, there is no failure in the kingdom of heaven, only growth and opportunity to try again.

But let me pause and address something I think is too important to not touch on at least briefly. You might be asking, *Are all people* really *God's happy place, even when they refuse to believe in Him, acknowledge His Son, Jesus Christ, or even when they commit the most heinous of human rights crimes?* I've struggled with that question while I worked with and for people who have suffered extreme persecution at the hands of others.

One of the most confronting times was when God called me back into refugee work in 2015. I was very unwilling, but I obeyed. I intensely disliked the work. It was stressful, and having worked in the field as a young lawyer, I knew the heartache it involved. As I stepped back in, I had to study atrocities recently perpetrated against others. I had to read and watch material the contents of which I've not shared with others due to how horrendous it was. My theology was rattled as never before. Could I in all honesty look at my clients who had suffered so much and say, "God is good, He adores you, but He also adores those who persecuted you"?

With tears coursing down my face, I sought God for answers. I understood the idea of free will, and I knew these people were using theirs to commit heinous crimes upon innocents. But then I felt God's love for all those who were victims *and* those who were perpetuating such wickedness. I felt His deep grief at the situation. All human beings *are* His happy place, but not all our behavior brings Him joy.

Sometimes we willfully disobey and bring grief to the heart of God. I believe His heart breaks as He holds the tension of loving all beyond measure as He witnesses what we human beings choose to do to one another. In the same way a parent doesn't delight when one child is cruel to another, so God doesn't always delight in us. However, we always remain in His love. It's clear that His wrath isn't for those perpetuating such villainy but for the forces behind such behavior (Ephesians 6:12). So, while we are all His happy place, not all behavior makes Him happy. Not all of us are streams that flow that make the city of God glad, but we all hold the potential to do so. I think the apostle Paul's transformation is a beautiful example to always remind ourselves of this truth.

But let's return to our role. What of the times when we, who believe in God and in Jesus Christ as His Son, choose not to obey? We might not willfully do evil, but what of the times we knowingly disobey? There might be a time when we feel we have nothing to give. What then? Are we God's happy place if *we* refuse to obey? Will His love still flow to us, for us, and through us to others?

I've learned that even when we feel empty, there's always more. Many times over I've discovered that if I will simply respond to God's nudge, there's always more than enough for both those I'm called to and me. Indeed, in allowing the streams of love to flow forth, love will come to us. Like a dry garden hose, if we turn on the tap to water another, we in turn will get wet. We will always be refreshed. But as a loving Father, God prefers we flow from a place of rest and overflow rather than from a place of perceived lack. So while we may feel empty, with nothing to give, it's simply not true. God's supply within is inexhaustible. His love will never end.

So through all the teaching, growing, and becoming is a profound truth to be realized. God will never love you any less if you choose to do nothing more than be the object of His affection. Turning your affection to Him, you will always be His happy place. But I suggest that to truly know Him yet not flow in His love is to not truly know Him. As I shared in chapter 1, it's His loving-kindness that leads us to repentance, to a changing of heart and mind toward ourselves, toward others, and most importantly, toward Him. It's His loving-kindness that causes us to learn and grow as a child of God.

TIME WITH GOD

The journey of love is complex, but yet so profoundly simple. We spend time with God, and we come to *know* that He is God (Psalm 46:10). As we soak in His love and bathe in His beauty, we change more into who we truly are. Imbued *in* His love, we become enticed to go, to show the world our lover, our Jesus. We choose to share Him with the world, and as we do, we get about the family business. As described throughout this book, an intoxicating transaction takes place.

We're in Him, and He's in us. We witness lives transformed as we respond to His heartbeat. Imbued in His love, we want to share God with those around us, and as we do, we can feel His deepest delight. We are the streams that flow from the river of God that make the city of God glad!

Yet life can get busy. People make many demands, and they covet your time and your prayers. You may find that as you live the life I describe, you begin to spend more time releasing His love and being about the Father's business and less time simply being *with* Him. In this place, you can grow weary. Life challenges, spiritual resistance—people draw on you. You love them and feel their pull, and while intellectually you know you *must* spend time with God, the world draws. Children, jobs, chores, tasks, bills, and commitments all demand attention, and somehow you may find yourself drifting from His embrace.

We all have challenges. I don't need to share my own, but I've had many. Somehow, like the woman in Song of Songs 2:10, my Lover came, and I didn't arise to meet Him. And when I heard the longing of my heart, I went to the Door and beseeched Him to enter, and I simply could not find Him. Yes, I was in Him, and He was in me, but my awareness of that sweet union was distant to me as I struggled through the days. And yet even in the place of weariness, as I sought Him in my heart, He was drawing me, teaching me, and wooing me.

I know He will do the same for you! Our choice to be with God and our choice to respond to His voice in obedience is simply that—a choice. So even if we don't take time to be still with God, there's always a flow available. That's because, truth be told, He abides in us, and we abide in Him. Nothing can ever separate us or remove us from that place of connection. Yet it's not ideal to ignore that intentional place of abiding. Even so, it was in this place of lack where I learned the most important lesson of all: I experienced God's deep love for me, and He showed me how His love for me will never end.

As I mentioned at the start of this chapter, I'm sure you've asked something like *Will God still love me if I don't obey? Will God still love me if I don't spend time with Him? If I know He wants me to do some-*

thing and I don't do it, will He still accept me? I hope you know the answer to this one, but do you *really* know?

Understanding that we should do something in a moment but not doing it. Getting all the "feels" as a prompt yet not acting. To disobey in the moment. What then?

GOD IS GOOD STORY: HIS LOVE WILL NEVER END

Years ago I was weary and tired. I had a happy, healthy, heavy toddler in a stroller and had driven half an hour to a shopping center to purchase ballet essentials for my daughter. I hoped to get in and out fast—to "bag it" and run.

Making my way through the center, I walked past a young man who had a perfume bottle in one hand and a paper sample strip in another. With a thick foreign accent and a big smile, he invaded my space. Backpacker or international student, I surmised.

He waved the perfume at me, and I shook my head, smiling. But then I felt the nudge. *Stop for him,* God said.

No, I responded. *I'm tired. I want to get in, get out, and go home. But if he approaches me again on my way out, I'll stop.* With that, I walked on, hoping I could avoid the man as I left.

Purchase made and ballet items in hand, I headed back, hoping the young man wouldn't approach me again. I hoped I'd "heard" wrong.

As I pushed the heavy but happy and healthy child in the stroller with a weariness threatening to overwhelm me, I noted the smiling, enthusiastic, perfume-wielding, accent-laden young man ahead. Girding myself, I pushed the stroller more resolutely and put my head down to charge. But out of the corner of my averted eyes, I saw him heading my way. I veered left and kept veering until there was no more "left' to go.

Cornered, I thought. I pleaded with God: *Ok, OK, he's approached me. I know I made a deal, but I just can't.* I was close to tears. I had stopped for so many, and I felt tired. I knew God wanted to reach out to him, through me, and yet . . .

The young man reached out his hand, speaking as he cornered me against a shop window. Yep. God had done a doozy! A rush of emotions flooded me. God's heart for him was intense, and there was such a compulsion to speak to him. Such an overwhelm of love.

Did I stop? I wish I could say I did, but, no, I veered away again and kept walking. And as I did, I felt God's heart break for the man I wouldn't stop for. A love so intense, a heart so for the one before me. It was a profound love, and yet, instantly, simultaneously, there was a flood of love for me. A warmth, a kindness, and a goodness reverberated through my being. The complete love, acceptance, and adoration I felt from God for me was extreme. I was feeling His heart break for the young man as I simultaneously felt and heard His word of love for me.

Gently, He said, *I love you. I'm proud of you. You are weary and tired. Yes, I wanted you to stop for this one, yet I love you regardless.*

God's words of love and acceptance flooded my being, and as His love poured over my weary heart and body, the reality that I didn't have to perform for His love sank deep. I already knew this, but I didn't *know* this. Love silenced the voice of condemnation as I leaned into what God said to me and as I *listened* to what He spoke.

I will *never* forget this moment!

To hold the "both/and," rather than the "either/or," is challenging. We must hold both in the tension of being real and authentic. There's the tension of both resting in Him always *and* being about the Father's business. But we can acknowledge our weakness as we lean into His strength. To carry the extreme love He has for the ones we walk past every day yet to know that we know He adores us regardless of performance is a powerful lesson to grasp in this time of social media likes, performance, and acceptance through behavior.

This message from God rattled me to the core. But in understanding and receiving it, I knew I was where He wanted me to be. I was home in His arms of understanding. I am first and foremost His girl, His beloved daughter, in whom He is well pleased (Mark 1:11). I can do nothing to earn His love because His acceptance is complete. His approval is mine. He loves me, regardless. His love will never end. I am forever His happy place.

So, too, is it for you! Understanding this is paramount to your identity in Jesus Christ. You aren't a human *doing* but a human *being*. Complex and adorable, just as you are, you are God's happy place, and His love for you will never end. And yet there is a call, and it's a privilege to hear and respond. To partner with heaven is sheer joy. *We* are the streams that flow from the river of God that make the city of God glad. We are forever God's happy place.

But when He moves on our heart for the one on the streets, at the workplace, in our clubs or our schools, and so on, there's a responsibility we're all called to. Can you see the "both/and"? He delights as we join Him in expanding the family business. He loves the world to Himself. We are His arms, so to speak, that open wide to embrace all who are lost. Ambassadors in a foreign land, we represent Him. His love is our armor; His acceptance, our embrace. He invites us to co-labor in His labor of love. There is an ease in the heavenly dance. *Take my hand, little one. Let me lead*, He whispers to all.

So it was His *love* that taught me more about Him and more about His love for me.

Freedom comes as Jesus imbues our being. Yes, He prefers our presence over our performance, and He loves us regardless, but He wants us to also step into all He has preordained for our lives on this earth. Either way, when we fail according to the world, we're free to fall forward into His arms, for God is truly the loving Father and His love will never end. As we lean in and rest our head upon our lover, He will speak in various ways: Mixing His communication to ever increasingly expose us to His love, while simultaneously showing us who we are, all the while guiding us in how to become more fully ourselves, more fully how heaven sees us, more fully infilled and imbued with Him.

We have a privilege. Our steps pave the way for streams to flow from the river of life that is Jesus Christ, and *we* make the city of God glad as we flow. Although we can never be sure of the impact if we respond to His call, we can always be sure of His love if we don't, for we are His happy place and His love will never end.

QUESTIONS TO CONTEMPLATE

1. Do you truly believe that God's love for you will never end, and do you act like it? Journal what you discover as you ask yourself why you do or don't believe. Give explanations and examples.
2. When have you felt God's discipline? What was it like, and how did it make you feel? Given what you've learned in this chapter, do you need to revisit the memory with God and ask Him for His viewpoint, understanding that His love for you will never end?
3. What times can you recall when God revealed His complete love for you? Those moments will be there; it's a matter of recognizing them. Write those times up in your journal and share your testimony with a friend.

RESPONSE TO THE REVELATION

- **Action Step 1:** Ask God to help you recall a moment when you felt you failed Him, and then ask Him to show you your "failure" through His eyes instead of your own. If you identify any condemnation, understand that only the enemy condemns. Silence the voice of condemnation and focus your attention back on God, then ask Him for His viewpoint of the moment instead. Journal what you discover.
- **Action Step 2:** This week make a decision that you will respond to God's leading throughout your day. Ask Him to highlight people He'd like you to stop for. Regardless of what you do, journal what happens and how your action or inaction felt and what voices you heard within. After each attempt, whether successful or not, ask God for His viewpoint and how He sees you in each moment. Journal *all* your experiences, not just the "wins."

LET'S PRAY

Father, thank You that Your love for me will never end. Let me know these truths deep within my heart. Thank You that I will always remain Your happy place. I acknowledge that I've not always said yes to Your plans and purposes for me. I am sorry. Please forgive me for choosing my own ways instead. And thank You for having only good plans for my life. I say yes to those plans and purposes.

Show me Your ways so that I might be a conduit of Your living waters and in being so bring great delight to Your heart. Help me rest in Your arms when required and go forth as You direct fully refreshed. I want to grow into all You have purposed me to be, so I say yes to Your guidance and loving correction. Most of all, I ask that I will know Your love more profoundly, because I know as I experience Your love I am changed into who I was created to be and can love others and You more freely. In Jesus' mighty name I pray, amen.

DO YOU KNOW JESUS?

Throughout this book you've read about being God's happy place, and you now know you don't need to be a Christian for Him to love you. God can't love you any more than He already does—completely, utterly, and with a thoroughness beyond measure! His love is a gift freely given. But for a gift to fully benefit the intended recipient, it needs to be accepted, opened, and explored. God's arms are wide open, ready for you to say yes.

The gift He desires most for you is to receive Jesus Christ, who made a way for you so that you can be free to have a relationship with Him. In Scripture, Jesus is described as "the door" through which we walk into the arms of Father God.

In this book you've also read many stories. Some were from the Bible, and others were from my own life. They all involve a loving God who would love you to fully grasp how long, deep, and wide His love is for *you*. And for you to start to understand God's great love, you need to know that, before the beginning of time, the Trinity—God, Jesus, and the Holy Spirit—made a plan. They knew that upon creating human beings and giving them charge over the earth they would come to believe a lie about God and His great love for them. The fallout of this belief was sin, which caused a schism to occur in humankind's relationship with God. The problem was not on God's end (He was still there loving us); the problem was on ours. We hid, and we continue to hide today. God's desire from the beginning was always family and for you to belong too!

Being omnipotent (all-knowing), God knew ahead of time that this was all going to occur. And so with the help of His Son, Jesus, together with the Holy Spirit, a plan was devised where Jesus would come to earth as a man, filled with the Spirit of God, to live a life that demonstrated God in human form. In this plan, Jesus would lay down His life as a sign of their great love for humankind. Upon dying, Jesus rose to life again, as God had pre-ordained (and as was foretold in over three hundred prophecies). He then took up His rightful place by His Father's side.

You may never have been personally introduced to Jesus Christ. You might have heard *about* Him, but never *met* Him for yourself. If that's the case and you would like to meet Him, I invite you to take a moment to pray. Your prayer doesn't need to be complicated. God will always meet you where you are, and He's more interested in your heart than all the technicalities. Also know that prayer is simply a conversation with God, so I'm inviting you to have a heart-to-heart with Him.

In Romans 10:9, the Bible explains that "if you confess with your mouth the Lord Jesus and believe in your heart that God has raised Him from the dead, you will be saved" (NKJV). It's pretty simple: believe, receive, and respond. From there, God does the rest.

A great prayer to pray is found in Nicky Gumbel's book *Why Jesus?*[1] It reads as follows. Why don't you pray this out loud with me now?

> *Lord Jesus Christ,*
> *I am sorry for the things I have done wrong in my life (take a few moments to ask His forgiveness for anything in particular that is on your conscience). Please forgive me. I now turn from everything that I know is wrong.*
> *Thank you that you died on the cross for me so that I could be forgiven and set free.*

> *Thank you that you offer me forgiveness and the gift of your Spirit. I now receive that gift.*
>
> *Please come into my life by your Holy Spirit to be with me forever.*
>
> *Thank you, Lord Jesus. Amen.*

Not long after Jesus' death and resurrection, the Holy Spirit was sent to be our comforter, teacher, guide, strength, and so much more. Remember this book's chapter on God spaces? A section of that chapter discusses how the Holy Spirit was poured forth at Pentecost, about fifty days after Jesus' resurrection. We can invite Him to be with us—and better still to fill us with His Spirit. In this way we can declare that the same Spirit that raised Jesus Christ from the dead is in us! The Holy Spirit empowers us to live a life with God. He is joy-filled, fun, and all-powerful. It's through the Holy Spirit that we're invited into the family of God, and He keeps us company as we walk out our days on earth.

If you would like the gift of the Holy Spirit, ask Him to fill you with His presence and make Himself known to you:

> *Father God, I ask You to fill me to overflowing with the Holy Spirit. Holy Spirit, I invite You to fill me up! In Jesus' mighty name I pray, amen.*

You may or may not have experienced something as you prayed the above prayers, but either way, if you confess with your mouth that Jesus Christ is Lord and believe in your heart that God raised Him from the dead, you are saved (*sozo'd*; see the chapter 1 discussion on the meaning of *sozo*).

I could explain so much more here, but for now, I simply say, "Congratulations! Your new life has begun."

Now it's important for you to reach out to someone you know is a believer in Jesus Christ or a local church to explain what's happened to you, and hopefully they can walk out the next few steps with you, like baptism. But whatever you do, I highly recommend reading the pamphlet *Why Jesus?* by Nicky Gumbel. Written with clarity, it will take you through the basics of what Christianity is all about, why we need Jesus, who He is, what He claims, and the purpose of His death and resurrection in our lives.

I also highly recommend you find a nearby Alpha course or look at the Alpha website, Alpha.org, to find a course near you or online. These courses were also written by Nicky Gumbel and are a great way to discover what Christianity is all about. The courses provide a safe space for you to ask all the questions you'd like to ask to understand more about becoming or being a Christian.

Other great resources are the *YouVersion Bible* app, which includes the Bible in multiple versions and languages; the book *A Radical Faith: Essentials for Spirit-Filled Believers* by James W. Goll; the book *What the Bible Is All About Handbook* by Henrietta C. Mears; and the *MessengerX* app created by John and Lisa Bevere.

Whatever you do, I remind you that whoever you are, wherever you are, whatever you've done, you are and will always be God's happy place!

NOTES

1. God Sees, Hears, and Knows

1. Many scholars believe the angel of the Lord is Jesus Christ in His pre-incarnate form.
2. Hagar encounters the pre-incarnate Jesus Christ by a spring in the wilderness. In John 4, Jesus encounters another woman by a well. Both women discover they are seen by God and encounter Jesus Christ, the eternal spring of living waters. Whatever wilderness we are in, Jesus Christ sees us and is there to guide, refresh, and encourage us into the fullness of our kingdom purpose.
3. Later we will explore the woman at the well in John 4 who has a similar encounter with Jesus, who redirects her back into her community and into the potential of her purpose in Him.

2. Feeling God's Attention

1. See *Daring Greatly* (2016) and *Atlas of the Heart* (2021) by Brené Brown.
2. These basic needs are explored in Gary Chapman's book *The 5 Love Languages: The Secret to Love That Lasts*, paperback (Northfield Publishing, 2014).
3. "Choreb," Strong's Exhaustive Concordance #2722. Derived from "charab" (Strong's 2717) meaning desolate, dry. Moses was in a dry place. Also known as "Horeb," which translates to "the mountain of the Lord."
4. Some scholars believe that Mt Horeb (the mountain of the Lord) is the same mountain as Mt Sinai. Mt Sinai is where Moses later receives the ten commandments—a place where Moses receives instructions from God.
5. 21st Century King James Version; American Standard Version; Amplified Bible, Classic Edition; BRG Bible; and many other versions. See biblegateway.com for various versions of Exodus 3:4.

3. God Encounters Are an Invitation to More

1. Matthew 14:17–20; 15:32–37; Mark 6:35–44; 8:1–8; Luke 9:12–17; John 6:5–13.

4. The Command to Be Still

1. Other places where we see Jesus withdrawing to spend time with His Father include Luke 5:16, Luke 6:12, Mark 1:35, and John 6:15 to name but a few. And of course, don't forget His prayers in the garden of Gethsemane in Mark 14:32.
2. Jeanne-Marie Bouvier de La Motte Guyon (commonly known as Madame Guyon).

NOTES

6. Abiding in My God Space

1. Dr. Diane Divett (PhD; MEd [counseling]; PGCert Health Science [Child & Adolescent Mental Health], BEd, Dip Teach, MRFI) is the originator and developer of Refocusing as a life coaching, life mapping, self-awareness theory and practice, including Refocusing as the counseling theory and practice. At the time of my hearing her speak, she was a senior leader of a church in New Zealand.
2. *Refocusing and God Spaces: A Holistic Counseling Theory and Practice* (Lambert Academic Publishing, 2011). A helpful book for the layperson is *God Spaces to Refocus* also by Dr. Divett, published on *Blurb*, 2018 (see https://au.blurb.com/b/9551089-god-spaces-to-refocus to purchase). For further details go to http://www.refocussing.com.

8. Changed in His Presence, Chosen for His Purpose

1. baptizō. Strong's Greek Lexicon G907.
2. baptizō. Strong's Greek Lexicon G907.

10. God Calls Me by Name

1. *Yada.* Strong's Hebrew Concordance #3045.
2. Bethany Hicks and Dan McCollam, *The Power in a Name: A Treasure Map to Your Identity and a Road Map to Your Destiny* (Prophetic Company, Inc., 2023), 74–75.
3. Ephesians 2:20; Psalm 118:22–23; Isaiah 28:16–17; 1 Peter 2:4; 2:6–8; Matthew 21:42; Isaiah 8:14; Acts 4:11; Romans 9:33.

11. Lovers and Workers

1. Revelation 19:7; Isaiah 62:5; John 1:12; Romans 8:15; Galatians 3:26; 4:6; 1 John 3:1–2.
2. Mark 16:15; Luke 14:23, Matthew 28:19–20; Acts 1:8.
3. In this passage, the Greek verb *hupantaó*, translated as "meet," implies intentionality and purpose in the meeting, whether in anticipation of a significant event or in response to an urgent situation. The use of *hupantaó* highlights the relational and typically life-changing quality of these meetings in Scripture. See Strong's Greek Concordance #5221. https://biblehub.com/greek/5221.htm

12. God's Love Never Ends

1. "Introduction to Australian Rules Football," https://usafl.com/intro#what.
2. Strong's Concordance H4148.

NOTES

Do You Know Jesus?

1. Nicky Gumbel, "Why Jesus?" (Alpha North America, 2008), 21.

ACKNOWLEDGMENTS

There are those in our lives for whom we feel such gratitude. Mentors, advisors, friends, family, and, of course, God—Father, Jesus, and Holy Spirit. While I hesitate to name some, I know I must, for to honor rightly is kingdom.

My first are Dayle and Greg Hooker. I thank you for nurturing me in my raw state nearly twenty years ago. Your encouragement set the stage, and your loving-kindness and guidance led me to others for whose lives I am so grateful.

I thank James Goll, a father in the faith, whose teachings (with his beloved wife, Michel Ann, and friend Beth Alves) unlocked my identity and unique gifting in the body of Christ. As James says, books and recorded trainings can mentor, encourage, empower, and equip, and that they did for me! I am also very grateful for your more recent live mentorship program through which I now have the honor of knowing you personally. You have championed me in such a generous way. I will never forget.

Then there are also the multitude of those—some now in the cloud of witnesses, some I know personally, others I have never met—whose lives have radically impacted my own. Among those, Graham Cooke—who prophesied my writing over a decade ago—and those whose teachings and books have influenced me profoundly. They include Bill and Beni Johnson, Kris Vallotton, Mahesh Chavda, and John Paul Jackson. I am also more recently grateful to Dan McCollum and Bethany Hicks. We stand on the shoulders of greats who go before. They are best honored by our absorbing and assimilating what they themselves have paid such a high price for, and then paying it forward, so others may also step into their unique God-given callings. To all of you, I give my heartfelt thanks.

A special thank-you must also go to Joseph Peck and David Sluka—both gentle, kindhearted ones who saw the gold in me and said yes to my God-given design. I thank and honor you. It's been a privilege and also humbling to have you champion me such as each of you have.

I now turn to my family—Andrew, Rebekah, and Matthew! The battle has been fierce to step into the prophetic words spoken fifteen years ago, but here is the first of many books so prophesied.

Andrew, I thank you for being our family's standard bearer, for reading endless *God Is Good Stories* and countless rewrites of this book. Your patience, belief, and love seem to know no end. I love you, and I am grateful to call you husband, lover, and friend. Rebekah and Matthew, both of you with your dad have paid a price as I pursued the Lover of our souls. Thank you for being there with me, from little ones to fully grown. You have encouraged me to stop for the one and to now write and chase down my own dreams, as you continue to pursue yours. I am proud to be your mum. It is delightful watching your *God Is Good Stories* unfold! Without the three of you and your yes to all on my and God's hearts, none of this would have occurred. I am so glad to call you family, and I look forward to what's next for us all. I love you and am proud of each one!

I must also mention my dear friend Karen Brough. You have been in my corner, cheering me along and celebrating every step along the way! Your love and friendship are precious beyond belief! Here's to our ongoing yes as we pursue the next writing project on God's heart. And a shout out to Ian Richardson for his assistance in hashing out a finer issue that got me stuck! Your and Helene's love shines.

Dad, thank you for communicating your love so effectively. And, Mum, I finished my first! Hugs—I miss you both!

ABOUT THE AUTHOR

BETH KENNEDY is a prophetic voice with apostolic grace who lives to awaken hearts to the radical love of God and activate lives into Kingdom purpose. After walking away from a successful legal and corporate career, Beth said yes to the Spirit's leading. For over fifteen years, she's been equipping believers to hear God's voice, live prophetically, and walk boldly in their spiritual identity.

She's not just a teacher—she's a mentor and a walking testimony of what it looks like to live fully yielded to heaven's call. Through Verve Ministries, Beth creates transformative spaces for prophetic people to rise, be restored, and move in the power of their true identity. Her gift isn't just revelation—it's activation. With a blend of gentle strength and fierce love, Beth brings clarity, breakthrough, and practical tools that empower believers to live face to face with God.

As an internationally accredited trainer with Prophetic Company Global and a member of the Bethel Leaders Network, she brings deep expertise to her teaching ministry. Beth has mentored under renowned prophetic teacher James Goll for five years and presently serves as a facilitator in his "Mentoring with James" program. She personally mentors people in Prophetic Mastery, her flagship mentorship program, and regularly presents for Empower 2000.

Beth's heart for authentic connection extends far beyond formal ministry settings. In her Melbourne neighborhood, where she has lived for close to thirty years, she continues to stop for the one—looking for divine appointments in everyday moments and living proof that this way of life isn't about perfection, but about presence.

Through her regular blog, daily social media content, and newsletters reaching thousands of subscribers worldwide, Beth creates accessible pathways for spiritual growth and prophetic development. Her authentic, down-to-earth approach makes the supernatural feel natural.

Beth and her husband, Andrew, live in Melbourne, Australia, and share two wonderful children, Rebekah and Matthew, who are each pursuing their unique Kingdom call. Together, their family demonstrates what happens when people choose to live fully alive to God's purposes.

To learn more about Beth and her ministry, visit www.VerveMinistries.com or connect with her @BethKennedyVerve on Facebook, Instagram, and YouTube.

www.ingramcontent.com/pod-product-compliance
Lightning Source LLC
Chambersburg PA
CBHW070534090426
42735CB00013B/2979